Electronic Dance Music DJs

Stuart A. Kallen

San Diego, CA

About the Author

Stuart A. Kallen is the author of more than 350 nonfiction books for children and young adults. He has written on topics ranging from the theory of relativity to the art of electronic dance music. In addition, Kallen has written award-winning children's videos and television scripts. In his spare time he is a singer, songwriter, and guitarist in San Diego.

For more information, contact:
ReferencePoint Press, Inc.
PO Box 27779
San Diego, CA 92198
www.ReferencePointPress.com

LIBRARY OF CONGRESS CATALOGING-IN-PUBLICATION DATA

Name: Kallen, Stuart A., 1955-
Title: Electronic dance music DJs / by Stuart A. Kallen.
Description: San Diego, CA : ReferencePoint Press, 2017. | Series: Collective biographies | Includes bibliographical references and index.
Identifiers: LCCN 2015042812 (print) | LCCN 2015044212 (ebook) | ISBN 9781601529664 (hardback) | ISBN 9781601529671 (epub)
Subjects: LCSH: Disc jockeys--Biography--Juvenile literature. | Electronic dance music--History and criticism--Juvenile literature. | LCGFT: Biographies.
Classification: LCC ML406 .K35 2017 (print) | LCC ML406 (ebook) | DDC 781.648--dc23
LC record available at http://lccn.loc.gov/2015042812

CONTENTS

INTRODUCTION

Beats and Heartbeats

One of the best jobs in the entertainment business might belong to the disc jockey, or DJ, who plays electronic dance music (EDM). Superstar DJs earn millions of dollars writing and remixing songs and performing them in front of thousands of adoring fans.

For a DJ, "performing" can mean different things. Most celebrity DJs write and sing their own songs and play keyboard synthesizers, guitars, or other instruments on their musical mashups. DJs also pair songs of other artists with their own unique mix of sounds. Most pull everything together in the studio before a performance—selecting songs, manipulating the tunes with various electronic tools, and then mixing them into unique sounds with propulsive dance beats. What the fans hear is the end result, a recording that reflects the unique rhythm and vision of the DJ. What the fans see depends on the DJ, but the bigger the DJ, the bigger the stage show. Tiësto fans, for example, can expect to see a glittery fireworks shower onstage while a breathtaking array of rainbow-colored laser lights illuminates the arena and the crowd.

Performing was more complex in the early days of EDM, when the DJ's basic tools were "two turntables and a microphone,"[1] celebrated in the 1996 song "Where It's At" by alt-rocker Beck. At the time, it was common for hip-hop DJs to connect a mic to an audio mixing console, along with two turntables spinning vinyl records. With this equipment the DJ could sing or rap lyrics while scratching, or moving the records back and forth by hand to create repetitive beats called loops. This technique, called beat-matching, is a multistep process, as communications professor Bernardo Alexander Attias explains:

> For the DJ who spins vinyl records, [beatmatching] requires physical training; the DJ must learn to listen simultaneously to two (or sometimes more) tracks playing at once. . . . The skilled vinyl DJ can have two records playing simultaneously at matched tempos, sometimes for minutes at a time, while adjusting the volume and [tone] of the tracks to blend them together seamlessly.[2]

DJ Tools

In the mid-1990s, the influential Canadian DJ Richie Hawtin earned a reputation for creating long, beat-heavy pieces using three or four vinyl records at once. However, turntables made for CDs, rather than vinyl records, have taken the guesswork out of beatmatching. With digital turntables, DJs can simply look at displays that indicate beats per minute (bpm) and turn a knob to sync the beats from several CDs.

"The skilled vinyl DJ can have two records playing simultaneously at matched tempos, sometimes for minutes at a time."[2]

—Bernardo Alexander Attias, communications professor.

The music sequencer is another digital tool in the DJ's arsenal. Sequencers are digital recording and sound-mixing workstations that can make unusual noises or recreate the sounds of pianos, organs, guitars, horns, drums, and other instruments. Sequencers allow DJs to record, edit, and manipulate the pitch and scale of notes using filters and effects. A sequencer can sample, or take a portion of a previously recorded song, and reuse it as an instrument in a different song.

DJs like deadmau5 rely on the Ableton Live music sequencer, designed to create sounds during live performances. With a music sequencer, the DJ does not need physical skills; deadmau5 created a firestorm of controversy in the EDM community when

When EDM first became popular in the 1980s, DJs played at underground raves, which were collective experiences that featured drugs as well as frenzied dancing. Today, EDM DJs perform at mainstream clubs and even stadiums because the music has gained wider acceptance.

he admitted as much in his blog: "I just roll up with a laptop and . . . hit a spacebar [which plays the music]. Ableton syncs the [beats] up for me . . . so no beatmatching skill required."[3]

EDM Styles

As confusing as DJ sound equipment might seem, perhaps nothing is as puzzling as the maze of genres and subgenres that define EDM. Although *EDM* stands for "electronic dance music," it is actually much more than that. According to DJ Moby, EDM is "a catch-all term for the different forms of electronic music."[4] Moby says that all EDM is based on beats per minute—and he would know. He set a Guinness World Record for fastest tempo in a single with his 1,000-bpm song "Thousand" (1993).

EDM genres, or styles, have colorful, evocative names. Among them are trance and psytrance, dubstep and thugstep, grime, happy hardcore, and moombahton. The EDM style known as house has a tempo of around 128 bpm. This mimics the heart rate of a person exercising. Trance music is faster, with a signature tempo of up to 150 bpm. Both styles adhere to a 4/4 drum pattern, similar to the beat of most rock songs. Other EDM styles are also classified by the number of beats per minute; deep house is slower than house, with 125 bpm. Psytrance is 146 bpm, and drum and bass is 175. Dubstep, a sound popularized by Skrillex, is 140 bpm. The dubstep sound also includes what are called breakbeats; the steady 4/4 rhythm is broken up by several independent drumbeats playing at once. This rhythm is called syncopation, cross-rhythm, or polyrhythm. Moby describes other complex musical elements present in dubstep:

> It's a descendant of Jungle [style], an early '90s, very fast form of EDM with Reggae . . . influences. Jungle morphed into Drum and Bass, and then there was an offshoot of that, two-step, which slowed the bass lines way down. Heavy Metal and Hip-Hop, interestingly, share the same tempo, around 75 bpm. Dubstep is an amalgamation of the two.[5]

Raves and Ravers

EDM originated in the late 1980s at underground dance parties called raves. Because illegal drugs such as marijuana, LSD, and MDMA (Ecstasy) were used at raves, the events were often held in secret locations such as abandoned buildings, empty storefronts, and open fields. Today EDM DJs play at lavishly decorated dance clubs, concert halls, and some of the biggest venues in the world, including football and soccer stadiums.

Rave fashions can be as over the top as the music, and ravers cast a wide net when it comes to style. Fashions are inspired by psychedelic hippie culture, goth, heavy metal, hip-hop music, and Japanese manga comic books. Ravers wear the colors of the rainbow, dressing in fake fur leg wraps, body chains, and shiny neon-colored dresses, pants, and vests.

Auditory Artists

Rave culture has helped make multimillionaire superstars of EDM DJs like Avicii, Calvin Harris, Skrillex, and others. But blinking lights, sequencers, and drum machines do not get people up to dance; it is the artistic mix of the DJ that can transport listeners to dizzying heights and slow them down to mellow moods. EDM journalist Hillegonda C. Rietveld describes the EDM DJ as a "party leader, sonic entertainer, auditory artist, music programmer, record mixer, beatmatcher, cultural masher, music producer, creative music archivist, record collector, sex symbol, role model, upwardly mobile brand, youth marketing tool, dancefloor parent, witch-doctor, [and] shaman."[6]

> "[The DJ is a] party leader, sonic entertainer, auditory artist, music programmer, record mixer, beatmatcher, [and] cultural masher."[6]
>
> —Hillegonda C. Rietveld, EDM journalist.

Rather than play music, EDM DJs create long, danceable tracks that are said to play the crowd. DJs push dancers to the limit, lull them into hypnotic trances, and rev them back up into states of near madness. Using state-of-the-art digital equipment, DJs trigger one of the oldest human desires—the urge to dance. And as any good DJ will admit, it is the audience that makes the show.

CHAPTER 1

Avicii

In May 2013 the twenty-three-year-old Swedish DJ Avicii stepped onto the huge main stage of Miami's Ultra Music Festival with a singer, guitarist, kazoo player, and banjo player. Fans at one of the world's biggest annual electronic music festivals were unimpressed. They booed. They tweeted insults. Avicii's "Wake Me Up," a bluegrass tune amped up by whizzing synthesizers and dance beats, was an immediate flop. But then something striking happened. About a month after the song's official release, it zoomed to the top of the charts in sixty-three countries. In the United Kingdom it became the fastest-selling single of the year. Within ten weeks a video of Avicii's performance of "Wake Me Up" had racked up more than 165 million YouTube views.

This was the reaction the hugely popular EDM DJ had expected all along. As he later told *Rolling Stone* magazine: "Bluegrass to me has always been something credible and kind of cool in the sense that it's very melodic."[7] The statement says a lot about Avicii. If a sound moves him, whether it is bluegrass or rhythm and blues (R & B), he is not afraid to experiment with the style. And although he likes to please his audience, Avicii does not have to worry about losing them. By the time "Wake Me Up" was released, Avicii was so popular he could afford to experiment. In 2013 he played around three hundred shows, sometimes earning $250,000 for a single appearance. In 2014 alone, Avicii earned more than $19 million.

Great Talent Being Born

Avicii, whose real name is Tim Bergling, is one of the richest super-star EDM DJs in the world; he is also among the youngest. Born in Stockholm, Sweden, on September 8, 1989, Avicii began writing and remixing tracks at age eighteen. As Avicii recalls, he was drawn to working on a computer because he found he had little talent for playing music: "I always wanted to make music or find an outlet for creativity somewhere. I had dabbled with guitars and piano but was never particularly good at it." A friend introduced him to a computer program that made it possible for him "to create melodies like a piano and I was hooked."[8]

> "I've always listened to everything. What defines my tastes is that it's always got to be melodic and hooky."[9]
>
> —Avicii, DJ, music producer.

Avicii was the youngest sibling in his family and heard a great deal of music growing up. He recalls, "My brothers and sisters were all about 15 years older than me and they were listening to hard rock and glam rock. . . . But I've always listened to everything. What defines my tastes is that it's always got to be melodic and hooky."[9]

The hookiest, or most attention-grabbing, music Avicii could find was produced by a Swedish EDM act called the Swedish House Mafia. The group—made up of Axwell, Steve Angello, and Sebastian Ingrosso—formed in 2007 and quickly became one of the most prominent names in house music. House music is an EDM style that originated in the early 1980s in African American dance clubs in Chicago and Detroit.

Swedish House Mafia and other EDM groups inspired Avicii to create house music on his laptop. One of his first tracks was called "Lazy Lace," a remix of music from the 1984 video game *Lazy Jones*. More tracks followed as Avicii often worked nine hours a day in his bedroom recording with CD turntables and effects boxes, which are used to add distortion, echo, and other sound effects. At times his parents were alarmed at what Avicii calls the "constant *donk-donk* thumping"[10] emanating from the bedroom. However, the results were noteworthy, according to EDM journalist Payal Patel: "His friends noticed that the productions were amazingly professional and that they had just witnessed a great talent being born."[11]

Winning the Fast Trax Competition

When Avicii posted his early tracks on the social network Myspace, he found that the user name Tim Bergling was taken. A friend suggested he take his stage name from the Buddhist word *Avīci*. The term denotes the lowest level of Buddhist hell; the dead who have committed the foulest deeds are cast into *Avīci*. Although the concept has deep meaning to Buddhists, Avicii chose the

Avicii is a highly respected and well-paid DJ who has worked throughout his native Europe and across the globe. His songs have earned him Grammy nominations in the United States and Top 10 spots on dance charts in the UK, Italy, Germany, Greece, Croatia, and other nations.

The Birth of House

Avicii is one of the foremost purveyors of house music, a style with roots in an unlikely mix of sounds that includes disco, soul, pop, Latin, and British synthrock. Although house music today is dominated by white, European DJs like Avicii, the sound originated with African American musicians performing at gay clubs in Chicago in the early 1980s and then quickly spread to Detroit, New York, and cities in the United Kingdom.

In New York City, black Brooklyn teenager Larry Levan spun records at Paradise Garage (where the "garage" music style emerged). Levan often shared the bill with DJ Frankie Knuckles, now known as the Godfather of House, who migrated to Chicago in 1977 to preside over the dance floor at the Warehouse (where the term *house* originated).

Early house DJs played disco, a genre that blended 1960s-style Motown soul, Latin music, and uniform rhythms produced by drum machines. House DJs used extended-play vinyl disco records that included long percussion breaks. While looping disco beats, house DJs mixed in soul vocals by Isaac Hayes, Grace Jones, and others, along with synthesizer sounds from British synthpop bands like Depeche Mode. DJs also added sound effects that had never been heard before. The result was a driving dance sound described by music journalist Barry Walters in 1986: "It goes BOOM BOOM BOOM BOOM with little variation, subtlety, melody, instrumentation—or music for that matter. . . . It's in the house, and it won't come out."

Barry Walters, "Burning Down the House: Read SPIN's 1986 Feature on Chicago's Club Scene," *Spin*, April 1, 2014. www.spin.com.

name because he thought it sounded cool. (He added the extra *i* because the name Avici was already taken on Myspace.)

Avicii got his first big break in April 2008 when he was still in high school. He entered the BBC Radio 1 DJ competition called Fast Trax, hosted by the celebrated DJ Pete Tong. His song "Manman" won more than 70 percent of the audience vote, which led Tong to sign Avicii to his Bedroom Bedlam record label. In the days that followed, Avicii was flooded with offers from record labels, talent managers, and booking agents.

Twenty-six-year-old Arash "Ash" Pournouri was one of the managers pursuing Avicii. The Iranian-born club promoter based in Stockholm was impressed by Avicii's ear for melody and wanted to take part in the EDM boom. Avicii met Pournouri for coffee, figuring the promoter could at least get him some club gigs. As

Avicii recalls, he was not prepared for what he heard: "He started saying all of these things like, 'I'm going to make you the biggest artist; we're going to get there in two years; you're going to be bigger than that guy and that guy.'"[12]

Taking Listeners on a Journey

Avicii signed up with Pournouri's At Night Management company, but there was one hurdle to overcome before he could be "the biggest artist." Avicii had never performed as a DJ and had no idea what the work entailed. Pournouri hired a few professional DJs to train Avicii, but it took about eighteen months for him to get comfortable in the DJ booth. As Avicii learned, much of the work is done on a computer long before the DJ gets onstage; set lists are predetermined and sound effects and song transitions preprogrammed. Although older DJs insist that they "read the room" or adjust the music to the energy in the audience as the set unfolds, Avicii does not believe they are really doing this: "[That sounds] like something a lot of older DJs are saying to kind of desperately cling on staying relevant."[13]

Like other DJs, Avicii does a lot of the sound mixing in the studio before a gig but controlling the audience's energy level is central to his act. And to do so, he spends much of his time onstage pushing volume sliders up and down to build the music to a spirited crescendo. Avicii believes his main job is to interact with the audience—smiling, waving, and pumping his fist to push dancers to the limits of their physical endurance. Pournouri even gave a talk on the subject called "The Avicii Case Study" at the 2012 Electronic Music Conference. As he explained: "A great DJ takes his audience on a journey. You want them so into it that *they can't leave*. The tracks that get the attention are the songs that create some kind of *feeling*."[14]

> "A great DJ takes his audience on a journey. You want them so into it that *they can't leave*."[14]
>
> —Ash Pournouri, Avicii's manager.

In the studio, Avicii found that magical feeling by laying down a typical 4/4 house beat, known as four on the floor. This rhythm underlies songs with lyrics his fans can relate to; he writes about love, emotion, personal setbacks, and desire. Above it all, Avicii mixes in echoing keyboards, whirling sound effects, and sirens. A random, unexpected pause gives a song a sense of substance or surprise. According to critic Rob Kapilow, these elements create a pleasing sound: "It's peppy, it's upbeat, it's got a steady groove. There's nothing not-smooth about this music, nothing to annoy you. This sort of repetition is very comforting; it's why children want to hear the same book over and over again."[15]

A New Level of Success

Avicii's fan base exploded in October 2011 when he released the upbeat song "Levels" (stylized as "LE7ELS"). The fist-pumping club anthem was an instant global hit, reaching number one in Sweden, the United States, the United Kingdom, and elsewhere. "Levels" defines the Avicii formula, with a four-on-the-floor beat and catchy, repetitive synthesizer licks. What makes the song unique is the gospel-tinged vocal by R & B singer Etta James, sampled from the 1962 song "Something's Got a Hold on Me." Avicii was thankful for James's contribution to his song, and after she died in January 2012 he recalled the generation-spanning qualities he heard in her singing: "It's timeless. She really has soul. . . . [I was charmed] by the power of her voice."[16]

In March 2012 the massive success of "Levels" helped Avicii land one of the biggest DJ gigs in the world. He was asked to headline the sold-out three-day Ultra Music Festival. The festival, attended by more than one hundred thousand keyed-up EDM fans, featured big-name acts like Skrillex, Afrojack, and David Guetta. But Avicii stole the show when he was joined onstage by pop superstar Madonna, who introduced Avicii's remix of her single "Girl Gone Wild."

In April Avicii landed starring gigs at Lollapalooza in Chicago and the Coachella Valley Music and Arts Festival in Indio, California. After a few weeks off, Avicii launched a seventeen-city North American tour backed by a dazzling, tech-infused stage production. Reviewer Elliot Alpern describes a June 2012 Avicii show in Pittsburgh:

> The Swedish house star performed from the summit of a gigantic white head that towered over the packed floor.

In June 2012, Avicii performed on a spectacular stage in San Francisco's Bill Graham Civic Auditorium. As part of his Le7els Tour, the show supported the release of his debut album. Just three months prior, he had headlined the sold-out Ultra Music Festival in Miami.

. . . Though it may have initially resembled some carved sculpture, the surface of the head was anything but static. With 3-D mapping technology, projectors were able to beam images onto the face, of which Avicii immediately took advantage. A pair of lipstick-smothered lips appeared on the face, mouthing the sampled Etta James lyrics of "Levels."[17]

A *True* Mad Scientist

Stardom in the EDM world made it possible for Avicii to produce his debut album, *True*, in 2013 with a nearly unlimited budget. He was also respected enough to attract top-name talent. For the album's first single, "Wake Me Up," Avicii enlisted neo-soul singer Aloe Blacc and Mike Einziger, lead guitarist in the alt-rock band

Incubus (both musicians debuted the song onstage at Avicii's 2013 appearance at the Ultra Music Festival). Legendary guitarist Nile Rodgers, founder in 1976 of the disco-funk group Chic, also collaborated on *True*. Rodgers and singer Adam Lambert cowrote and performed on the track "Lay Me Down."

Perhaps the most unusual collaborator on *True* was the seventy-one-year-old songwriter Mac Davis, who wrote "Addicted to You." Davis is legendary for the Elvis Presley hits he wrote in the 1960s, including "In the Ghetto" and "A Little Less Conversation." But Davis claims he loves EDM—and he was also very impressed by Avicii: "He's a genius, no getting around it. I'm a traditional songwriter. I put my guitar in my lap and sit there for half a day. To watch him work, I swear, is like watching a mad scientist, with his computer and his focus."[18]

> "[Avicii's] a genius, no getting around it. . . . To watch him work, I swear, is like watching a mad scientist, with his computer and his focus."[18]
>
> —Mac Davis, musician and songwriter.

True contains the usual EDM sound samples, synths, drum machines, and filtered, robotic vocals. But the album also features acoustic guitars, twangy electric guitar leads, and Blacc's earthy voice. As music critic Philip Sherburne notes, this led some to accuse Avicii of "going country,"[19] including stunned audiences who heard "Wake Me Up" at the Ultra Music Festival. However, the album samples many traditional music genres, including disco, alt-rock, pop, and 1960s soul music. Sherburne describes the results: "*True* feels as family-friendly as any Disney picture, and that's no slight. . . . Avicii has made an album with the kind of pure pop heart that's as likely to appeal to eight-year-olds as it is to amped-up ravers."[20]

Working Hard

Avicii's meteoric rise to fame has come with a price. The stress and lifestyle of a world-renowned EDM DJ has taken a toll on his health. In 2013 he spoke publicly about his struggles with alcohol addiction. He says his drinking is a result of being unprepared for the hectic life of a touring performer: "You are traveling around,

The Difficult Side of Stardom

Before achieving worldwide fame, Avicii released a song called "Alcoholic." Toward the end of the upbeat house song, Avicii repeats a phrase: "Call it what you want I'm . . . [an] alcoholic." The lyrics revealed a personal side of Avicii—one that has taken a toll on his career. In 2013 Avicii admitted to a reporter that he is an alcoholic. He said he began drinking too much when he first started touring Sweden in 2008 at age eighteen. He blamed his problem on the temptation posed by free alcohol at backstage parties.

Avicii's drinking has affected his health. In 2012 he was hospitalized with severe abdominal pains in New York. In 2013 he was stricken with acute pancreatitis in Australia. The painful condition, which is rare for someone in their twenties, causes fever, nausea, and vomiting. The problem forced Avicii to cancel his scheduled tour of India that same year. The most serious issue occurred in 2014, when Avicii collapsed before his scheduled third annual appearance at Miami's Ultra Music Festival. Avicii was rushed to the hospital, where doctors removed his gallbladder. In September 2014 Avicii canceled the remainder of his concerts in order to regain his strength.

Quoted in Philip Sherburne, "EDM Superstar Avicii Made a Kazoo-Heavy Kinda-Country Record with 'True,' It's Awesome," *Spin*, September 12, 2013. www.spin.com.

you live in a suitcase, you get to this place, there's free alcohol everywhere. . . . I just got into a habit, because you rely on that encouragement and self-confidence you get from alcohol, and then you get dependent on it."[21]

Drinking has seriously affected Avicii's health and landed him in treatment centers and hospitals more than once. Alcohol-related health issues forced him to cancel all of his scheduled concerts in the latter part of 2014.

Although Avicii chose to stop touring, he did not abandon his music; by the time he canceled his shows, he had written seventy new songs. And in 2014 he announced that his second album, *Stories*, would include more big-name acts, including Jon Bon Jovi, Wyclef Jean, and Coldplay's Chris Martin. By March 2015 Avicii was on the road again, performing at Australia's Future Music Festival. Whatever the ups and downs of his life, Avicii attributes his success to fate and dedication to his art: "I never dreamed of making music on this level, or touring on this level. You know, it has all happened fast. But I worked really hard."[22]

CHAPTER 2

Annie Mac

It is no secret that male DJs dominate the world of EDM. This was decisively demonstrated in 2014 when the electronic music website Thump studied the male-female ratio of DJs booked for the upcoming EDM summer festival season. The study showed that of the 184 acts performing at the Electric Daisy Carnival in Las Vegas, 5 were women. At the Electric Zoo festival in New York City, there were 3 women performers among the 116 acts.

With women making up only around 2.5 percent of all working DJs, Annie Mac has beaten the odds. Mac performs at internationally renowned clubs and festivals, hosts the influential *Annie Mac* EDM show on BBC Radio 1, and produces the Lost & Found dance festival in Malta. But do not ask Mac what it is like to be a female DJ, or a pregnant DJ, or a DJ and a mother. She is fed up with interviewers asking these kinds of questions. "As far as I know 'DJ' is a genderless word. . . . The tools it takes to DJ—the technical knowhow, the crowd perception, the music knowledge—these are human tools. DJs are all just human beings playing records to people."[23]

Wanting to Be a DJ

Annie Mac was born Annie MacManus on July 18, 1978, in Ireland's capital city, Dublin. She comes from a family of musicians.

Her brother Rod MacManus is a skilled guitar picker and folk singer. Her brother Davey MacManus was a singer and songwriter who played with the British indie band the Crimea before moving to Africa to care for AIDS patients. Both brothers influenced Annie's early musical tastes, playing Irish punk, rock, and traditional folk music. She says, "I know every Pogues song by heart. I grew up properly in love with Thin Lizzy. There was always [traditional] stuff like The Furies and Christy Moore playing."[24]

When Mac was eighteen years old, she attended Queen's University in Belfast to study English literature. While studying for her degree, she came to love creative writing, poetry, and film. She also fell in love with dance music at a university club called Shine, located in the Student Union building.

Shine was one of Belfast's hottest techno music clubs, and Mac learned about it from one of her teachers. As she later commented: "It turned out that my English language lecturer—a proper [East London] Cockney geezer—worked there—it was all through English that I started my club career."[25] Mac heard many popular EDM DJs at the Shine, including Andrew Weatherall from the United Kingdom, Choice from France, and DJ Sneak and Green Velvet from the United States.

> "As far as I know 'DJ' is a genderless word . . . DJs are all just human beings playing records to people."[23]
>
> —Annie Mac, EDM and radio DJ.

While searching for electronic music on the radio, Mac discovered BBC Radio 1, an internationally broadcast station based in London. From the moment she heard the station, she set a goal for herself: "I wanted to be a Radio 1 DJ."[26] To achieve this dream, Mac bought turntables and a mixer and used them to remix old soul and funk records she purchased in thrift stores. In 1998 Mac's ambition drove her to move to southeastern England, where she studied for a master's degree in radio at Farnborough College of Technology.

When Mac's brother Davey formed the Crimea, Annie got her first gig as a DJ; she mixed music when the band took a break. When Davey moved to London in 2000, Mac followed. She soon found work at a small radio station interviewing bands for the

Student Broadcast Network, a company that provided music programs to student radio stations in the United Kingdom.

Mac's radio work helped her land a DJ gig at a London nightclub called the Underworld. The club attracted a mixed group of dancers with eclectic musical tastes, as Mac recalls: "You'd get every type of person in there from little skater boys, indie kids, punks, loads of tourists. Literally every walk of life was represented so it was a real lesson in keeping the dance floor full."[27] Mac rose to the challenge by mixing pop, hardcore, alt-rock, and other assorted sounds.

The Annie Mac Show

Working the dance floor at the Underworld did not deter Mac from her ultimate goal of landing a gig as a DJ on BBC Radio. Whenever she had time, she scheduled meetings with radio executives who might help her advance her career. However, things started off slow; Mac was hired to answer phones at the BBC headquarters in London. But in February 2002, Radio 1 producer Rhys Hughes gave Mac a chance. She was given a two-week stint as a temporary broadcast assistant for DJ Steve Lamacq, whose show *Lamacq Live* was the premier indie rock program on BBC Radio 1.

Mac's main task was producing short ads for Radio 1. Her first ad, for a punk rock radio program, was a hit with producers; they liked her Irish accent, which made the word *punk* sound more like *ponk*. Mac was asked to stay on as an assistant. While she continued to make ads, Mac observed radio DJs like Lamacq and others at work, and she learned about music, broadcasting technology, and the ways a successful DJ controls the pace and energy of a show.

While working as an assistant, Mac continued to push for her own show. She presented her bosses with recorded demos that showed off her skills with the turntables and microphone. In 2004 Radio 1 executives were impressed enough to allow her to have her own show. *Annie Mac* ran from 7:00 to 10:00 p.m. on Fridays. After landing the show, Mac stated: "To be honest, I really want to do this for the rest of my life."[28]

Mac used her position as a radio personality to present underground, or little-known, music to a wider audience. On her debut program, the twenty-six-year-old Mac played a variety of EDM, including the electronic synth sounds of the British group the Prodigy, the underground electronica of DJ Mylo, and the hip-hop electro house of American DJ Afrika Bambaataa. Her show took off; renamed *Annie Mac's Friday Night*, it was still attracting devoted listeners through 2015.

Annie Mac makes an appearance at the 2015 Brit Awards in London. In the late 1990s, Mac was studying English literature at Queen's University in Ireland when she was first introduced to the EDM scene. She then moved to London in 2000 to become a successful radio DJ.

Clubs, Radio, and TV

For some DJs, hosting a popular EDM radio show would be enough, but Mac was not ready to give up deejaying in the dance clubs. About a year after launching her radio show, she started hosting *Annie Mac Presents*, a DJ showcase at the London club fabric. The show, which featured sets by Mac and up-and-coming DJs, attracted a large audience. According to *Mixmag* magazine, *Annie Mac Presents* was "one of the biggest brands in clubland providing a platform for a generation of youthful, bass-driven, live-dance acts and making Annie herself one of the most in-demand club/festival DJs on the planet."[29]

> "[*Annie Mac Presents* was] one of the biggest brands in clubland . . . making Annie herself one of the most in-demand club/festival DJs on the planet."[29]
>
> —Mixmag, *EDM and club culture magazine.*

In 2006 Annie Mac wanted to reenact the nightclub experience for radio listeners. This led to the production of the *Big Weekend Dance Party*, broadcast live from London Nightclub Dundee. In addition to Mac's live performances, the show featured two hours of live performances by Mylo, Fergie, and Pete Tong.

Mac's musical expertise was also in demand on other BBC Radio shows. She often sat in on an arts program called *The Culture Show*, playing new EDM and offering her opinions on the hottest new DJs. Mac also crossed over to television in 2006, appearing on the music trivia game show *Never Mind the Buzzcocks*. She hosted the iconic British music show *Top of the Pops* and worked as a guest host on the MTV2 show *Gonzo*.

Annie Mac Presents

In 2009, to further her goal of showcasing unknown artists, Mac released a compilation CD called *Annie Mac Presents*. The album was like listening to an Annie Mac mix tape. It featured her favorite sounds of the year, including Dizzee Rascal, Twizzle, and Duck Sauce. *Annie Mac Presents* was so successful that she released a new compilation annually. The albums feature the year's best sounds, including widely popular club anthems,

The Dual DJ

There are two types of DJ. Radio DJs are announcers who pick records to play on the airwaves. EDM DJs mix beats, instruments, records, and other sounds at clubs, raves, and concerts. Whereas most DJs are one type or another, Annie Mac works as both an on-air radio DJ and an EDM DJ. This artful mix of occupations allows Mac to DJ at major EDM festivals while also pumping up the careers of newcomers on her *Annie Mac's Friday Night* radio show.

In 2015 Mac began hosting a two-hour "new music" radio show four nights a week. This allowed her to move beyond EDM and expose her listeners to hip-hop, rock, pop, and even folk music. Some of her long-time fans complained that Mac had abandoned EDM. But Mac was pleased with the new direction: "I'm more than just the 'dance girl.'. . . I'm excited by whatever doesn't fit in that box. . . . [I] play music I love and hope others invest in my opinion. I need not overthink it." This does not mean Mac is giving up the DJ booth anytime soon. She continues to work the biggest EDM festivals while playing all kinds of music as a radio DJ personality.

Quoted in Eve Barlow, "Annie Mac: 'I'm More than Just the Dance Girl,'" *Guardian* (Manchester), June 13, 2015. www.theguardian.com.

mellow moments, and never-heard-before tracks. Mac commented on the 2012 version of *Annie Mac Presents*:

> It's a good physical thing that is an [advertisement] for everything I'm about musically. I also love putting music together and having it as a memento for that year; the nice things about these compilations is that each one is roughly representative of a year in music for me. . . . I've really covered everything that I love and there's a lot of up-and-coming people on there but [also] a lot of exciting established people. . . . [The CD] is basically a DJ set that you would hear if you came to see me at a festival this year—that's why it was so natural for me to put it together.[30]

The release of the *Annie Mac Presents* CDs coincides with an annual DJ tour of the same name. At the live shows, Mac demonstrates her broad knowledge of EDM, which includes a wide variety of genres, including jungle, house, garage, and dance.

Life on the Road

For any touring DJ, famous or not, life on the road is not often glamorous. Most of the time is spent in motel rooms and airport lounges or on long drives on dark highways. Twitter accounts like @DJsComplaining contain a catalog of complaints about stolen equipment, lost baggage, bad Internet connections, and unpredictable road managers.

In 2013 Mac wrote an article for the EDM website Thump about her DJ travels during the previous decade. When she first visited the United States and Canada, she scheduled ten or twelve gigs in a row so she could make it back to London to host her weekend radio show. Mac picks up the story:

> I would cram in as many cities as I could . . . [with] every new day bringing a new hangover, a new airport and a few new pounds with each portion of chicken wings and cobb salad I consumed. They were tough tours. You would be lucky to break even, but they were such an adventure. One night you would be playing to twenty-

five people in Montreal, and the next to two thousand in NYC. It was always unpredictable and despite jet-lag, delirium and sometimes chronic loneliness, always interesting.[31]

Mac notes that the hours a DJ keeps can be grueling, especially while hosting a weekly radio show. For example, Mac has played the Ultra Music Festival on the Spanish island of Ibiza every year since 2010. The gig typically requires her to leave London on Thursday at 10:00 p.m., arriving on the island at 1:00 a.m. She performs onstage from 2:00 to 4:00 a.m., then flies back to London at 10:00 a.m. After a few hours' sleep, Mac arrives at the Radio 1 studio for her 10:00 p.m. Friday night show.

Annie Mac Sees Gender as a Nonissue

As a popular female DJ, Annie Mac is repeatedly asked the same questions about her gender. Mac often surprises interviewers with her answers. For example, when Mac is asked what it is like to be a female DJ in a male-dominated field, she responds that she has never experienced sexism. When she was just starting her career, she says, male DJs supported her efforts: "People seemed to be delighted that I was a woman out there doing my thing. . . . Not one male DJ has ever made me feel different or small because of my gender."

After she had a baby in 2012, Mac was often asked about the difficulties of mixing motherhood with a DJ career. Again Mac wonders why she is being asked this question. She often tells music journalists that being a DJ mom is no different than being a DJ dad. In fact, Mac says she gets parenting pointers from her male DJ friends. Like anyone who travels for business, Mac misses her child and her child misses her. As she says, "that is a very normal working situation for any parent who works away from home, male or female."

The most persistent question Mac hears is, why there are so few female DJs? Mac responds: "There are . . . loads of female DJs. Open your eyes. And your ears. They are coming through like wildfire. When you meet them, please for the love of God don't ask them about being female."

Annie Mac, "Annie Mac: Stop Asking Me Questions About Being a Woman," Thump, November 13, 2014. https://thump.vice.com.

No Boundaries

Mac temporarily stopped traveling when she had a baby in 2012, but she soon resumed touring. She longed for the joyous feeling of spinning tunes for fans but also feared losing her position as one of the top female DJs. As Mac described it: "I didn't work for four months. It was terrifying having to step down from a career that I'd been building for 10 years."[32]

> "One night you would be playing to twenty-five people in Montreal, and the next to two thousand in NYC. It was always unpredictable."[31]
>
> —Annie Mac.

To maintain her momentum, Mac not only continued to play numerous EDM festivals but also increased her presence on the radio. In 2015 Mac began hosting Radio 1's new music show, which runs Monday through Thursday from 7:00 to 9:00 p.m. And she continued to host her Friday night show. American EDM fans could listen to *Annie Mac Presents* on the Sirius XM radio station BPM. The chance to fill the airwaves with many more hours of music thrilled Mac: "The thing I love about music radio is those private epiphanies [moments of insight] it provides. Having 11 hours of airtime a week to share those moments with music that has no boundaries, is beyond a job, it's a privilege."[33]

Mac has long celebrated music with no limitations and has watched the dance music scene get bigger every year. And with her promotion of underground and up-and-coming DJs, there is little doubt that Mac has brought new audiences to EDM. She has also expanded the EDM sound by mixing together numerous genres and subgenres. As Mac says: "A lot of DJs now don't just play dub-step or house . . . they'll play garage and techno, bass music and jungle and hardcore and everything. And . . . it's gonna make people like really diverse music which I think is a really good thing."[34] EDM got its start in the United States, but with more than 1 million listeners every Friday night, Annie Mac has expanded EDM's reach throughout Great Britain, Ireland, and beyond.

CHAPTER 3

Afrojack

Afrojack might be one of the hardest working DJs in the EDM business. Since his breakout 2010 club smash "Take Over Control," Afrojack has toured extensively through North and South America, Africa, Europe, and Asia. He often plays three hundred concerts a year. When he is not on the road, Afrojack spends long hours in the studio. His devotion to his work is clear when one considers how he spent his summer a few years back. In 2012 Afrojack spent two weeks recording tracks with big-name artists like LMFAO and Flo Rida. He spent the next four weeks working fourteen-hour days at a Hollywood studio, where he perfected tracks he had already recorded. As soon as that was done, Afrojack wrote and produced an entirely new batch of songs. With all of the work he produced that summer, Afrojack was involved in every step of production—composing music, writing lyrics, and laying down tracks in the recording studio. As he put it, "When you come up with good concepts for songs, you have to put a lot of time and effort into it."[35]

Afrojack is often listed as one of the top ten DJs in the world, worth an estimated $40 million. He is a towering figure in more ways than one; he stands 6 feet 9 inches (206 cm) tall in his size 15 shoes. He travels the world in a private jet; collaborates with megastars like Beyoncé, Madonna, and Snoop Dogg; and briefly dated wealthy socialite and TV personality Paris Hilton. His life was not always this glamorous. Afrojack traces his roots to a modest suburban apartment in the Netherlands.

"Sort of an Outcast"

Afrojack was born Nick Leonardus van de Wall on September 9, 1987, in Spijkenisse, a suburb of the port city of Rotterdam. His mother, Debby, who is Dutch, owned a local gym. His father, whom he never knew, is of African descent, from the South American country of Suriname. Van de Wall loved music at an early age and learned to play piano when he was only five.

Van de Wall was a good student who could excel if he put his mind to it. However, he felt like an outsider in the largely white Dutch community where he lived. So he spent a lot of time with his music. As he recalls: "I was always like sort of an outcast. And when I got home [from school], I was always doing music, but when I was doing music, no one was there to judge it, you know? It was just me in my bedroom. It gave me freedom and made me happy."[36]

> "When I was doing music, no one was there to judge it, you know? It was just . me in my bedroom. It gave me freedom and made me happy."[36]
>
> —Afrojack, DJ.

When he was eleven, Van de Wall downloaded a music production software program from the Internet and began creating EDM mixes on his computer. He landed his first DJ gigs at age fourteen, playing fifteen-minute guest sets in local pubs. Patrons did not initially appreciate Van de Wall's underground sounds, which were mixed only from his own favorite songs.

To appeal to audiences, Van de Wall started mixing in popular songs. Pub goers particularly liked "Satisfaction" by Benny Benassi, a song considered a forerunner of the electro house style, with distorted voices run through a speech synthesizer. Watching the audience responses, Van de Wall learned something: "Nine out of ten people are not open to completely new things. . . . [But if] innovative elements are wrapped up in something which is quite familiar, then people can accept them."[37] Since that time, he has made a point of mixing little-known songs with popular ones. In this way he straddles the line between underground and mainstream while drawing fans from both camps.

After completing high school, Van de Wall attended classes in graphic design for a year. However, he felt he knew more about computers and graphics software than his teachers. In addition, the annual tuition was a lot of money for Van de Wall's mother. After dropping out of school, Van de Wall worked temporarily as a website designer for local DJs.

One of the hottest DJs in demand, Afrojack has collaborated with musical superstars such as Madonna and Snoop Dogg. He also finds time to work as a producer, songwriter, composer, and performing DJ. His productive work ethic has made him both popular and extremely wealthy.

The Storyteller

Afrojack sees himself as a storyteller. But rather than use words or lyrics, he uses music to tell stories. He views a repeating melody much like a character in a story—with the rising and falling of the tune representing the character's actions. Below he gives an example of how the character, represented as a melody, leaves home, goes out to experience an exciting adventure, and then returns home.

> After about a minute [of music] the character is announced. And then the story begins. It slowly builds up until there occurs a sort of explosion. They call it the drop. Then the bass [kicks] in, strengthening the theme. Then there are chords. Layer by layer it builds further on. There's more bass on, and everyone goes wild. Yes, and he finally comes home again. As a DJ, you can extend the story endlessly. The [CDs on the turntables] are the actors and you decide what they do.

Quoted in Maarten van Rossem, "Afrojack, Businessman Between Underground and Mainstream," *Maarten!*, February 19, 2013. www.maartenonline.nl.

Doing the Dance

By the time Van de Wall turned eighteen, he was regularly performing short sets in Rotterdam nightclubs. Hoping to broaden his audience, he went to Greece, where he worked as a DJ from 8:00 p.m. to 5:00 a.m., six nights a week. His weekly pay was the equivalent of about $250. In 2006 he moved back to the Netherlands, where he booked short gigs in five different cities every weekend.

In January 2007 Van de Wall released his first single, "In Your Face," using Afrojack as a stage name. He took the first part of his name from the long, curly Afro hairstyle he wore at the time. He says the second part refers to his electrifying, jacked-up beats. (Afrojack now sports a buzz cut and says that the Afro made him look like a gigantic tree when combined with his elevated height.)

"In Your Face" is a good example of electro house with a prominent kick drum beat and a tempo of 130 bpm. Although the song failed to make the charts, Afrojack's next single, "Drop Down (Do My Dance)," recorded in 2008 with DJ production team the Partysquad, reached number one on the local dance charts in the Netherlands. The song remained on the charts for seven weeks.

The hard-driving electro house of "Drop Down (Do My Dance)" helped Afrojack book gigs at major dance festivals, including Amsterdam's Sensation festival and Belgium's Tomorrowland, which is one of the biggest EDM events in the world. While working these festivals, Afrojack was able to meet some of the biggest names in the music business, and this led to several high-profile collaborations. In 2010 Afrojack worked with EDM superstar David Guetta on the song "Toyfriend" and was invited by Lady Gaga to remix her song "Alejandro." His work on Madonna's hit "Revolver" won a Grammy Award for Best Remix in 2011.

Taking Over Control

Afrojack released his breakthrough single, "Take Over Control," in 2010. The song was cowritten by and features the vocals of Dutch singer-songwriter Eva Simons. With its infectious beat and repetitive synth lines, the song was a club hit, reaching number one on *Billboard*'s Hot Dance Airplay charts and staying there for six weeks.

Simons also starred in Afrojack's first official music video for "Take Over Control." The video was filmed in Mojave, California, at an airplane graveyard filled with hundreds of junked commercial airliners. Being a producer rather than a performer suits Afrojack just fine. He likes making music and being behind the camera more than being in front of it. As he explains: "Eva was amazing. She was like a superstar doing the dance moves, doing the singing. She was great at it. I'm a producer. I make music. I'm a nerd. So with the video . . . she can do the singing and the dancing."[38]

Working with Pitbull

With a hit single and video attracting international attention, Afrojack's star continued to rise. In March 2011 he collaborated with Miami rapper Pitbull on the hit single "Give Me Everything," which also features R & B singer Ne-Yo and Latin pop singer Nayer. Afrojack's production provides a club-ready mix of hip-hop and electro house driven by up-tempo drum kicks, sizzling synths, and airy blended vocals by Ne-Yo and Nayer on the sing-along chorus.

With more than 8.2 million in sales, "Give Me Everything" was among the top fifty best-selling singles of all time in any genre. The song hit number one on the *Billboard* Hot 100 in the United States and topped the charts in Canada, Belgium, Ireland, and the Netherlands while reaching the top five in twenty other countries. In 2015 the video of "Give Me Everything" attracted nearly 7 million hits on YouTube.

Despite its success, the song was panned by numerous critics, including Shahryar Rizvi, who wrote:

> "Everything" provides a mosquito synthesizer noise that will worry all the dogs in your neighborhood. . . . It's so jumbled that it's relatively difficult to distinguish this track from similar Top 40 house-influenced tracks. . . . After a while, you start to hear the difference, sure; it's Ne-Yo repeating the word "tonight" in the chorus, which is something that gets annoying really fast.[39]

He Cannot Be Stopped

Afrojack does not worry about critics he calls "haters." He says that his music is from the heart and people love it because it is genuine. Afrojack's belief was confirmed in the United States during his 2012 American festival tour. In March he performed to the screaming, pogoing ravers at Miami's Ultra Music Festival, sometimes accompanied onstage by his then-girlfriend Paris Hilton. The crowd hung on every fat bass line as Afrojack debuted the new track "Fatality" and incorporated some of his newer material, including "Take Over Control" and "No Beef" (featuring electro house DJ Steve Aoki and singer Miss Palmer). The grand finale was a live rendition of the powerful chart-topping single "Can't Stop Me Now," performed with the vocal group Shermanology.

> "[The Afrojack song] 'Everything' provides a mosquito synthesizer noise that will worry all the dogs in your neighborhood."[39]
>
> —Shahryar Rizvi, music critic.

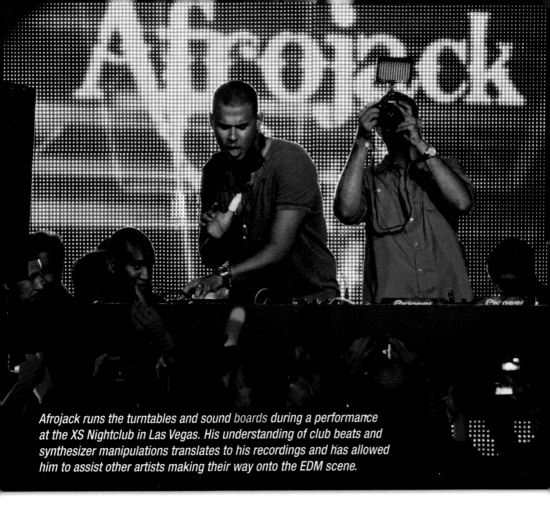

Afrojack runs the turntables and sound boards during a performance at the XS Nightclub in Las Vegas. His understanding of club beats and synthesizer manipulations translates to his recordings and has allowed him to assist other artists making their way onto the EDM scene.

Afrojack followed the Ultra Music Festival with an appearance before seventy-five thousand EDM fans at the Coachella Valley Music and Arts Festival in California. During Afrojack's finale, he was joined onstage by rock legend Paul McCartney and R & B megastar Usher, both of whom pumped their fists and danced.

Afrojack played forty more North American gigs after Coachella, including a stint in Las Vegas, where he earned $150,000 for a single night at the XS Nightclub. Afrojack considers Las Vegas his second home, a place where huge new dance clubs like XS, Hakkasan, and Omnia have opened since 2012. The clubs try to outdo one another with opulent interiors, laser light shows, suspended performance platforms for dancers, floor-to-ceiling LED screens, and even two-story waterfalls. As Afrojack told one interviewer, "Vegas is like Disneyland for grownups."[40]

Afrojack Loves His Cars

Afrojack loves fast, expensive cars, and with earnings of more than $22 million a year, he can afford them. In 2013 he crashed his brand new Ferrari 458 Italia just forty-four minutes after driving it out of the showroom. Luckily, he was driving relatively slowly, 45 miles per hour (72 kph), when he hit an oil slick and spun out. He posted pictures of the smashed $240,000 sports car on his Twitter feed but said he was sad that he wrecked such a beautiful car: "Cars for me are like a piece of art. Even though I was really happy that I was completely fine and alive . . . I also felt bad that I just wrecked an art piece."

Afrojack's next purchase was a $400,000 Lamborghini Aventador. About a week after buying the car, he was racing a friend on a Dutch highway when he was pulled over for driving 105 miles per hour (169 kph). He claims he was actually driving 125 miles per hour (200 kph). His license was automatically suspended for this blunder.

Without a license, Afrojack was forced to let his driver take the wheel. In 2014 he was chauffeured around in his $300,000 Rolls Royce Ghost. In addition to housing a V-12 engine with a top speed of 155 miles per hour (250 kph), the Ghost has a custom Afrojack touch: The car's classic Spirit of Ecstasy hood ornament disappears with the touch of a button and is replaced by an ornament with Afrojack's logo, a sweeping letter A.

Quoted in Zack O'Malley Greenburg, "A Spin with Afrojack: Inside the Dutch DJ's Car Collection," *Forbes*, October 20, 2014. www.forbes.com.

Sparking Dynamite

Soon after the tour ended, Afrojack began work on his first studio album, *Forget the World*. Throughout 2013 he built excitement for the album by releasing four of its singles. The first track, "As Your Friend," released on iTunes in February 2013, was a collaboration with R & B and hip-hop recording artist Chris Brown. The progressive house single with hiccupping synths and electronically altered vocals quickly rose to number one on the *Billboard* Hot Dance Club Songs chart. The video, which features Afrojack, eagles, and female dancers, attracted more than 25 million views on YouTube in 2015.

In October 2013 Afrojack released a second single, "The Spark," featuring vocalist Spree Wilson. Afrojack's next single, "Ten Feet Tall," with vocals by Wrabel, gained considerable positive notice when it debuted in a 2014 Super Bowl XLVIII Bud Light commercial seen by 100 million viewers.

Afrojack seemingly saved the best single for last, dropping "Dynamite" in April 2014, a month before *Forget the World* was released. "Dynamite" features aggressive lyrics by renowned rapper Snoop Dogg. Afrojack added his usual electro house elements, propelling the song with double time kick drum beats. The soaring, cinematic strings add musical elements of the trap genre, which features multilayered synthesizers and ultra-deep bass lines.

Forget the World featured collaborations with rock star Sting and rapper Wiz Khalifa. When discussing the album's title, Afrojack said he wanted to send a message to his fans and to himself. *Forget the World* is a reminder to ignore outside pressures and find inspiration within. As Afrojack explains: "Always remember to keep following your heart, keep following your path, and never try to let the things around you get you down. . . . You're going to be way happier doing what you actually love and finding other people that love the same thing than doing something that other people love."[41]

> "Always remember to keep following your heart, keep following your path, and never try to let the things around you get you down."[41]
> —*Afrojack.*

Building a Beautiful Future

Afrojack showed the world one of his inspirations in 2013 when he posted on YouTube a twenty-minute video documentary about his life. In the video, Afrojack talks about his two-year-old daughter, Vegas (from a previous relationship with Dutch model Amanda Balk). Afrojack describes the difficulty of spending so much time away from Vegas and reflects on his life: "I love making music and creating an amazing, energetic show for the crowd, but the love of my life is my daughter. In this career I have to make a lot of sacrifices and one of those is not getting to be with her all of the time. Being away from my daughter is hard, I hate it, but I know that by me doing this now I can build a beautiful future for her."[42]

As part of that beautiful future, Afrojack built a huge home on 15 acres (6 ha) of forested land between Amsterdam and Rotterdam. Although he could live anywhere in the world, he chose the site because it is close to his mother, and he enjoys living among, as he puts it, "normal, hardworking people."[43]

> "I want my Grandma to be able to listen to it and understand."[44]
>
> —Afrojack.

Also on the property is a full recording studio that includes a speaker system that cost hundreds of thousands of dollars, and a sleeping loft so he can work on his music for hours on end. Afrojack has always been a hard worker, and that has not changed. Neither has the goal he set for himself when he was just fourteen: to produce sounds never heard before and mix them with catchy music to grab the attention of the largest audience possible. As he said about his music in 2012: "I want my Grandma to be able to listen to it and understand."[44]

CHAPTER 4 — Skrillex

The EDM superstar Skrillex is one of the most widely heard DJs in the world. He has sold millions of chart-topping albums and holds numerous Grammys and other music awards handed out by Teen Choice, *Billboard*, and MTV. Skrillex's music videos have earned billions of hits on YouTube.

In live performances at sold-out arenas, Skrillex mixes up a stylistic history of dance music. He brings in old-school elements from 1970s disco, layers in 1980s electro and house music, and drops in beats from 1990s glitch, a style that uses sounds previously considered unwanted noise. Skrillex mixes all these genres together with dubstep, a genre pioneered by London DJs in the early 2000s. The original dubstep sound is sometimes called wub-wub music for its aggressive wobbling bass lines, which give the music a menacing feel. The style also features samples of Jamaican reggae songs driven by a powerful, syncopated dance beat.

To his fans' delight—and his critics' dismay—Skrillex restructured dubstep to make it more palatable to American teenagers. He moved the style away from its gritty Jamaican roots and warped it into an aggressive dance-metal hybrid. Music reviewer Robert Ker describes the Skrillex sound: "His tracks draw from

Skrillex is known for mixing a variety of dance beats with electronic screeches and other harsh noises. The resulting dance metal is likely a legacy of his roots in the rawness of punk rock and the aggressiveness of scream.

disparate strains of dance music—progressive house, electro, dubstep, glitch—and mash them together in fidgety, stuttering stew, with catchy melodies interrupted with violent bass drops—sub-woofer screams land like bombs and dissolve in distorted low-end howls, reminding listeners of movie monsters."[45]

A Scruffy Coder

Skrillex concerts attract hordes of young people dressed in neon-colored outfits who dance, pogo, and throw their arms in the air for hours on end. But Skrillex, who stands 5 feet 4 inches

(163 cm) in his stocking feet, might seem like an unlikely celebrity. Music journalist Jonah Weiner describes Skrillex's appearance when he is not onstage: "His stringy black hair drapes over a rumpled black T-shirt, and the left side of his skull, typically shaved clean in what has become his iconic look, has grown wooly with neglect . . . [he] resembles a coder deep into a marathon programming binge."[46]

> "Sub-woofer screams land like bombs and dissolve in distorted low-end howls, reminding listeners of movie monsters."[45]
>
> —Robert Ker, music reviewer.

The comparison to a programmer who writes computer code is appropriate. Using digital instruments such as drum machines, turntables, synthesizers, samplers, and sequencers, Skrillex mixes sounds with the same precision a coder might use to create a website. But he is more than that. He is also a musician; he was playing bass guitar and singing in a punk band by age fourteen.

Anger and Screamo Music

Skrillex was born Sonny John Moore on January 15, 1988, in the Highland Park neighborhood of Los Angeles. When he was two, his family moved to San Francisco but moved back to Los Angeles when he was twelve. Moore's father worked for an insurance company; his mother was a homemaker. Both parents belong to the Church of Scientology, but Moore does not identify with the religion, founded in 1954 by science-fiction writer L. Ron Hubbard.

In 2004, at age sixteen, Moore discovered he was adopted. It was not a happy time. In a 2014 interview with *Rolling Stone* magazine, he described his feelings at the time: "Whether my parents forgot to tell me, or didn't know when the right time was, I didn't find out till I found out randomly. And I was angry. Who wouldn't be?"[47] When he later learned that a woman he knew as a family friend was actually his birth mother, that hurt even more. (Skrillex has not seen his biological mother since he was a teen, nor his biological father since 2008. Today he says his adoptive parents are "dope."[48])

Moore often fought bitterly with his parents after he learned the circumstances of his birth. His anger led him to drop out of high school and search for ways to escape his life at home. While surfing the social network Myspace, Moore learned that a Georgia-based band called From First to Last needed a singer. With his parents' permission he traveled to Georgia, where he was hired as the band's new lead vocalist. It was 2004 and From First to Last was already in the process of recording its first album, *Dear Diary, My Teen Angst Has a Body Count*. Moore provided the lead vocal tracks on the record. He also sang on From First to Last's second album, *Heroine*, which was released in 2006.

From First to Last played a brand of music known as post-hardcore and screamo. Post-hardcore combines heavy metal guitar licks with the flailing drums of punk rock. And screamo, as the genre name indicates, relies on anguished lyrics that are screamed, shrieked, and yelled. In 2012 Skrillex recalled why the style fit his mood perfectly at the time: "I was angry, so I kind of just said forget everyone and made some music that was angry music. But I'm not an angry person."[49]

> "I was angry, so I kind of just said forget everyone and made some music that was angry music. But I'm not an angry person."[49]
>
> —Skrillex.

From First to Last toured extensively, and by 2006 the concerts had taken a toll on Moore's voice. He developed masses of tissue (nodules) on his vocal cords; these growths resulted in painful hoarseness, breaks in his voice, and made it impossible for him to sing. Moore required two operations to remove the nodules. Soon after the second surgery Moore quit From First to Last and moved back to Los Angeles to pursue a solo career. He was happy to be on his own, as he told *Rolling Stone* magazine in 2014: "It was one of those situations where people did not get along. . . . Bands are great, but I couldn't express myself in that band."[50]

Going Solo

The move from a live band to electronic music seemed natural. Moore had been listening to EDM acts like Aphex Twin and

From First to Last

Five years before Sonny Moore adopted the name Skrillex, he was hired as lead singer in the Georgia-based band From First to Last. The band's sound was inspired by heavy metal and hardcore punk. Those sounds were combined with an aggressive offshoot of emo called screamo. Although emo and screamo both feature confessional lyrics that touch on emotional pain and unrequited love, screamo is characterized by short, dissonant songs with shrieking vocals.

From First to Last's 2004 debut album, *Dear Diary, My Teen Angst Has a Body Count*, featured Moore screaming at the top of his lungs over churning guitars and propulsive drumming. The album reached number twelve on the *Billboard* Heatseekers Albums chart.

From First to Last released its second album, *Heroine*, in 2006. The gritty album with soaring choruses and obscene lyrics received good reviews and peaked at number twenty-five on the *Billboard* 200. That same year, the group performed concerts in North America and Europe. However, Moore's screaming took a toll on his voice, and he was forced to quit the band when he had vocal cord problems. From First to Last released several more albums without him, including 2015's *Dead Trees*.

Squarepusher since he was thirteen. Aphex Twin is the stage name for Irish-born DJ Richard D. James, whose dreamy, atmospheric ambient techno brought him fame in England in the early 1990s.

Moore's early electronic music combined these EDM influences with his rock background. He gave his synthesizers a harder, rock edge and combined them with punk drums and electric guitar riffs. The blend may be heard in the three songs, "Signal," "Equinox," and "Glow Worm," that Moore released on his Myspace website in 2007.

While playing with From First to Last, Moore had developed a substantial fan base. His new music attracted the same kinds of fans—those who love screamo. This crossover appeal is still part of what drives his success, as events promoter Ryan Jaso explains: "He's kind of a gateway drug. He's brought all these kids who like metal and hard rock . . . over to the electronic dance music scene."[51]

Moore proved that alternative rock fans would be drawn to his music when he started touring as a solo act. In 2007 he performed on the Team Sleep tour, fronting for alt-rock bands such as Monster in the Machine and Strata. In early 2008 Moore continued to work the alt-rock circuit as part of the sold-out AP Tour promoted by *Alternative Press* magazine.

My Name Is Skrillex

In April 2009 Moore released his first solo extended play, or EP album, *Gypsyhook*. The nine-song album features Sean Friday on drums, percussion, and drum machine. Moore sings and plays all the other instruments, including the guitar, bass, keyboard, synthesizer, turntable, sampler, and music sequencer. The electro-pop sound of the album, overlaid with strange lyrics, attracted the scorn of critics. As Joe DeAndrea wrote on Absolute punk.net: "Throughout the EP, the vocals continually get worse. They're incredibly grating and headache inducing, so the only redeeming quality is when it's just the music playing, but even that eventually gets boring."[52]

Although it is unknown what Moore thought of such criticism, he did change his name and image. By the time *Gypsyhook* dropped, Moore was using the stage name Skrillex at Los Angeles DJ gigs. When asked about it, Moore states that Skrillex was both his AOL Instant Messenger alias and his nickname: "[It] really means nothing. Throughout my teen years my friends would call me 'Skrillex' or 'Skril' or 'Skrilly.'"[53]

After assuming a new name, Skrillex adopted his trademark hairstyle, one that evolved from the long hair he grew as a teenager to cover his serious acne. Skrillex picks up the story: "I used to hide my face with my hair all the time. That's why I have long hair. [But] I shaved the side of my head as a kind of a way to get over that. I was like . . . 'now I can't hide my face! I'm not here to be pretty. I'm here to make music.'"[54]

To draw attention to his new pseudonym, he called his next EP *My Name Is Skrillex*. The twenty-eight-minute, six-song al-

> "[The vocals are] incredibly grating and headache inducing, so the only redeeming quality is when it's just the music playing, but even that eventually gets boring."[52]
>
> —Joe DeAndrea, music critic.

bum was released for free on Skrillex's Myspace page. The EP attracted the attention of progressive house music DJ dead-mau5, who released the second Skrillex EP, *Scary Monsters and Nice Sprites* on his mau5trap record label.

Production of *Scary Monsters and Nice Sprites* did not take place in the usual studio setting. Skrillex recorded the CD's nine tracks in his apartment on his laptop computer. The informal, low-tech setting did not seem to hurt the sound. *Scary Monsters and Nice Sprites* provided the breakthrough Skrillex had been searching for. The single "Kill EVERYBODY" became an instant club hit, and critics loved the album. Reviewer Max Paradise was among those who praised *Scary Monsters and Nice Sprites*:

> The music takes a sharp left turn with the jaw-dropping title track. Starting off with an absolutely gorgeous synth melody, Skrillex brings in his trademark aching chopped up vocal samples, before suddenly hitting listeners over the head with . . . the heaviest dubstep drops. . . . But Skrillex manages to work so much melody and throbbing beauty into his dubstep, it's hard to think of his work on the same plane as his peers.[55]

Scary Monsters and Nice Sprites hit number one on *Billboard*'s Heatseekers Albums chart and number three on its Dance/Electronic Albums charts. In 2011 *Scary Monsters and Nice Sprites* won a trio of Grammy Awards, including Best Dance/Electronica Album and Best Dance Recording. By 2013 *Scary Monsters* had sold more than 2 million copies, and the title track was played more than 210 million times on YouTube.

In 2011, while deejaying an astounding 322 concerts, Skrillex continued to record and produce original music. He released *More Monsters and Sprites* in June and *Bangarang* in December. As he had done with *Scary Monsters*, both were made available for free on the Beatport website.

Keeping Fame in Perspective

As a celebrity DJ and music producer, Skrillex tries to keep his fame in perspective. As he stated in early 2012: "I never try to

Dubstep and Brostep

Dubstep is the foundation for Skrillex's chart-topping sound. The style, which originated in London in the early 2000s, was the leading style heard in European dance clubs in 2010 when Skrillex released his EP *Scary Monsters and Nice Sprites*. However, Skrillex changed the gritty dubstep sound, lightening it with lilting piano chords, ethereal vocals, and swirling synthesizer riffs. He also added cartoonish original touches like squeaky helium vocals, stadium rock hand claps, and video game bleeps and buzzes.

Scary Monsters and Nice Sprites helped make dubstep a mainstream sound, especially after the album grew in popularity at college fraternities in the United States. However, the album was criticized by dubstep traditionalists, who derisively referred to Skrillex's Americanized style as "brostep." To critics, brostep is sanitized dubstep, a cleaned-up, soulless sound aimed at fist-pumping frat boys. With his usual sense of humor, Skrillex turned the slur into a song, "All Is Fair in Love and Brostep." He called it "the hardest, most over-the-top, dope . . . brostep song ever."

Quoted in Jonah Weiner, "The Boy Inside the Beat," *Rolling Stone*, March 27, 2014, p. 37.

overthink things. I just try to shut everything else out and make records that I like. I don't like hype cluttering art."[56] This attitude has not stopped Skrillex from working with one of the most hyped artists in the music business. In 2012 he was commissioned by Lady Gaga to remix some of her biggest hits, including "Born This Way," "Alejandro," and "Bad Romance." Skrillex has also remixed songs for the Black Eyed Peas and produced songs for the nu-metal band Korn. And the DJ gigs continued; in 2012 he earned $15 million playing to more than 250,000 people at 150 shows in 19 countries.

Skrillex is known for his strong work ethic. In 2011 and 2012 alone he produced numerous music videos, founded his own record label, composed an award-winning song for the animated film *Wreck-It Ralph*, and created a track for the video game *Syndicate*. In order to get everything done, something had to give. Usually it was sleep. Skrillex says he often slept only a few hours a night while recording music on his tour bus between gigs. And, despite some speculation about drug use, Skrillex insists: "I don't do hard drugs. . . . People always say it must be some cocaine lifestyle, but nobody could sustain that and do all the shows I do."[57]

An Alien Ride to *Recess*

Skrillex's days of producing music on the fly came to a halt in 2013 when he moved into a luxury loft in downtown Los Angeles that doubles as his home and recording studio. While Skrillex was busy mixing his next album, *Recess*, a team of engineers

Toting a guitar instead of standing in a DJ booth, Skrillex performs at the Bonnaroo Music and Arts Festival in 2014. His set list at the festival featured songs from his recently released album Recess, *including "Try It Out," "Fire Away," and the title track.*

worked to create a Skrillex video game app called *Alien Ride*. In the app, users control a spaceship to destroy asteroids. The app also contained a mysterious countdown clock. When the countdown reached zero on March 10, 2014, the first song on *Recess* was available to stream through the app. Every thirty minutes another song was made available, until all eleven songs were released.

Recess proved to be Skrillex's highest-charting album to date in the United States and the United Kingdom. It debuted at number four on the *Billboard* 200 chart and was later included in *Rolling Stone*'s 50 Best Albums of 2014.

Even before the release of *Recess*, Skrillex had been the target of numerous detractors on Internet message boards. He was accused of watering down the aggressive dubstep sound to attract a wider audience. Critics began describing Skrillex's signature style as "brostep" because it of its appeal to college fraternity brothers (or "bros"). Skrillex answered these charges with humor; the first track on *Recess* is called "All Is Fair in Love and Brostep." When asked about what he calls "haters," Skrillex simply says: "I don't have much time for the internet. I go to shows and all I see is love. I didn't even know people had an issue until someone said: 'Oh, [some people] seem to have a real problem with you.'"[58]

Thinking Back

Skrillex turned twenty-seven in 2015, and he had much to celebrate. In little more than five years, he managed to detonate a dubstep explosion that conquered America while attracting millions of new fans to EDM. He plays to crazed crowds nearly every day of the week, and his name is searched for on Beatport fifty times more often than any other DJ.

Through it all, Skrillex remembers his roots and seems to be humbled by his success. As he told British music critic Joe Muggs: "There is nothing better, than once in a while being with my friends [on tour] in a suite that's almost bigger than the houses any of us grew up in, and thinking back to the little festivals we would do in LA, or the punk shows we would go to, and thinking . . . 'this music that I never even meant to be released got us here.'"[59]

CHAPTER 5   deadmau5

d eadmau5 might be one of the least recognizable superstar DJs in the world. deadmau5 (pronounced "dead mouse") only appears onstage wearing a giant mouse head helmet, and few fans know his face. But deadmau5's brand of progressive house music has put him in the top ten on every best DJ list in the world and has earned six Grammy nominations. deadmau5 commands more than $100,000 per show and has a net worth of more than $45 million.

Rolling Stone magazine calls deadmau5 EDM's first true superstar. But he does not like being called a DJ and often rolls his eyes when he hears himself described as one. deadmau5 feels the term *DJ* is hopelessly outdated and does not come close to describing what he does. Unlike most DJs, deadmau5 does not prerecord his shows from sampled CDs made by other artists. During his live performances deadmau5 mostly plays music he has composed; he assembles tracks spontaneously as the night unfolds, using cutting-edge technology powered by software that he himself wrote. As deadmau5 explains: "There are no CDs involved. . . . If people come out to see deadmau5 I want them to hear deadmau5 music."[60]

Video Games and Computers

deadmau5 was born Joel Thomas Zimmerman on January 5, 1981, in Niagara Falls, Ontario, Canada. His mother, Nancy, is an artist; his father, Rodney, was an auto worker at the General Motors plant. Zimmerman has an older sister, Jennifer, and a younger brother, Chris.

According to Nancy, when he was around five years old, Zimmerman developed a sense for dangerous mechanical mischief. He would send sparks flying by sticking a fork in an electrical outlet or run a magnet across the television set to create a distorted image while causing permanent damage to the old-style picture tube. Zimmerman's grandmother, Katherine Johnson, fostered this behavior when she bought him a set of precision electronics tools for Christmas. Additionally, Katherine purchased old appliances like toasters and TVs at thrift shops and encouraged Zimmerman to take them apart and put them back together.

Katherine also bought Zimmerman his first Atari video game. Nancy remembers leaving for work in the morning and seeing Zimmerman playing *Minesweeper*. When she would return eight hours later, he would still be glued to the screen, surrounded by scraps and crumbs of half-eaten meals. Zimmerman later honored his first Atari with tattoos on his arm depicting the pixilated, old-school graphics produced by the machine.

Perhaps to tear him away from his Atari, Zimmerman's parents enrolled him in piano classes, which exposed him to classical music. Although he took lessons for eight years, Zimmerman says he hates classical music and cannot remember how to play piano. He was far more interested in the Intel 486 PC his uncle gave him. Although the machine was very primitive, Zimmerman learned to produce blips and beeps on it using basic programming skills. And as he said in 2011, the minute he touched the 486, "electronic music was in the cards for me."[61]

"A Little Weirdo"

When Zimmerman was a teenager his parents divorced, an event that motivated him to become a rebel. He dyed his hair bright yellow and shaped it into spikes. He wore sagging phat pants that showed off his boxers and a necklace made of plastic bouncy

In his signature mouse-face helmet, deadmau5 performs at a Las Vegas event in 2012. While other DJs typically shuffle through other artists' CDs during their live sets, deadmau5 prefers to amaze audiences with his own music, often created on the spot using computers and synthesizers.

balls like those found in a toddler's playpen. Nancy wanted to encourage Zimmerman's creative new style but was worried. As she told *Rolling Stone*, "Joel kind of isolated himself and was even ostracized, because he was a little weirdo, a little nerd. . . . He wasn't social and he still isn't. He lives in his computer."[62]

Zimmerman found one place where he would not face derision; he began attending rave parties, where DJs played EDM all night long. Although Zimmerman's tastes ran more toward the industrial rock of Nine Inch Nails, raves were the main social events for teenagers in southern Ontario in the mid-1990s.

The Dead Mouse Guy

In 1995 Zimmerman's love of video games and computers came together with the introduction of *Impulse Tracker* software. The program, called a digital sound tracker or music sequencer, allows users to produce music tracks. Zimmerman used a computer in his mother's basement to create his own video game music on *Impulse Tracker*. He also produced chiptunes—musical compositions made from sound chips, or integrated circuits, used in old computers and game consoles. The chips make simple electronic noises that can be used to produce repetitive musical segments called loops. The loops can be layered together on *Impulse Tracker* to create sound effects such as those used in the late 1990s by industrial rock acts like Marilyn Manson.

> "He wasn't social and he still isn't. He lives in his computer."[62]
>
> —Nancy Zimmerman, deadmau5's mother.

Zimmerman's computer skills led to his first job after high school. In 1998 he went to work for a low-budget dance music radio show in Niagara Falls called *The Party Revolution*. Since he was the only person in the studio who knew how to use a computer, his official job title was "technical whiz kid." Zimmerman helped the DJs digitally record their work. He recalls: "I overtook them when it came to technology. I learnt about digital audio and making music on computers, new editing techniques. Every new bit of technology that was released to do with making music, I was on top of it, while they were still dinosauring it out playing on turntables."[63]

Zimmerman tried to find work at local record companies, but no one at the time seemed interested in digital recording. Few studio engineers understood the possibilities of the relatively new technology.

In 1999 Zimmerman left Niagara Falls and moved 80 miles (129 km) north to Toronto. He convinced the owners of a house music label, Play Records, to install a few computers and used them to record local bands. His dream at the time was to work as a producer, helping musicians create original music. For his own enjoyment Zimmerman wrote electronic music that used synthesizers, drum machines, samplers, and sequencers.

Canadian Raves

During the mid-1990s, when deadmau5 was still a teenager named Joel Zimmerman, rave parties were ubiquitous in southern Ontario where he lived. Reporter Sarah Liss describes the rave scene that enticed deadmau5 and thousands of other Canadian teenagers:

> Teens and 20-somethings would travel to remote hangars and cavernous event spaces in yellow school buses, and wear fairy wings or elephant-legged pants or home-sewn overalls made out of bedsheets. To some, the appeal of raves was a revitalization of the daisy-chain ideals of hippie culture; party kids would scrawl the motto P.L.U.R. (peace, love, unity, respect) on their forearms with neon high-lighters so the letters would glow under black light. To others, the scene represented pure escapism—it was an excuse to drop ecstasy [MDMA or Molly], get blissed and zone out. Rave culture was simultaneously a space that allowed young adults to revert to an infantile state (complete with baby pacifiers as accessories), a seedy underworld that offered risk and rebellion to bored feckless youth, and an expansion of the urban nightclub scene into the suburbs and beyond.

Sarah Liss, "How deadmau5—a.k.a. DJ Joel Zimmerman—Came to Make $100,000 a Show and Have Four Million Facebook Fans," *Toronto Life*, November 1, 2011. http://torontolife.com.

Zimmerman's salary at the record label was only $1,000 a month. The rent on his run-down apartment was $800 a month, and Zimmerman sometimes went hungry. However, the experience provided him with his deadmau5 stage name. One of the numerous mice living in his apartment crawled into a partially disassembled computer and was electrocuted. When Zimmerman told the story to his coworkers, they started calling him the dead mouse guy. He embraced the name but shortened it to deadmau5, because deadmouse was too long to use in the Internet chat rooms where he spent his free time.

Hooking Listeners

Zimmerman uploaded some of his chiptunes to the chat rooms, and they came to the attention of Tommy Lee, the drummer for Mötley Crüe. Lee was looking for some new sounds to put on his solo rap-metal album *Methods of Mayhem* (1999) and ended up using some of Zimmerman's chiptunes. Lee and Zimmerman have been close friends ever since.

Luck played a role in Zimmerman's next big break. In 2006 he was talking to a friend, Steve Duda, about how easy it is to create a house track. To prove it, Zimmerman and Duda produced "This Is the Hook." (A hook is a repetitive instrumental passage or vocal melody that makes a song appealing and easy

Hiding behind his mouse-head mask, Joel Zimmerman prefers anonymity while performing as deadmau5. Having criticized the EDM industry for being more concerned with money than music, Zimmerman remains an outsider among his superstar peers.

to remember.) "This Is the Hook" was meant to be something of a joke. The song includes overused EDM ingredients: chugging synth lines, straight-ahead four-on-the-floor drums, and instruments passed through digital filters to color the sound with tones instantly recognizable to dance music fans. To ensure listeners got the joke, a robotic voice describes the clichés as they appear on the track: "Now is the time for the breakdown. . . . Let's filter the highhat. . . . Let's filter the chords."[64]

"This Is the Hook" was posted on Beatport under the name BSOD (an acronym for "blue screen of death," computer jargon for the blue error screen displayed on Windows operating systems). Zimmerman and Duda were shocked when the song rose to number one within days. As Zimmerman later stated, he realized he should take the music more seriously: "It was at a time when I was pretty financially strapped. . . . Money was pretty tight. We were like, If we can make some money doing this, we should play along with it."[65]

Zimmerman's next song, "Faxing Berlin," was released in July 2007 under the stage name deadmau5. Zimmerman did not leave anything to chance with this release. He sent the song to Pete Tong, one of Britain's best-loved dance DJs. Tong played "Faxing Berlin" on his influential BBC Radio 1 *Essential Selection* show, and the song quickly rose into Beatport's top ten. "Faxing Berlin" contrasts a speedy house beat with a dreamy minor-key trance melody, and listeners were enthralled by deadmau5's innovative fusion of styles. The song generated a host of imitators, prompting deadmau5 to comment: "It was quite a buzz to know that I'd influenced the course of dance music."[66]

> "It was quite a buzz to know that I'd influenced the course of dance music."[66]
>
> —deadmau5.

Creating a Mouse Head

deadmau5 produced several more attention-grabbing tracks, including "Sex Lie and Audiotape" and "The Reward Is the Cheese." These were released under deadmau5's new record label, mau5trap. deadmau5 created the company logo on his computer, pairing a demented, grinning mouse head with oversized ears.

While viewing the logo using 3-D software, deadmau5 came up with his next big idea. He decided to create a giant mouse head to wear during DJ gigs, which were multiplying in number due to his growing fame on Beatport. deadmau5 believed a mouse head would set him apart from other DJs and transform him into a mainstream icon. He contacted a Toronto film prop company to build a mouse helmet, or what he calls a mau5head. The first time he wore a mau5head, at a club in Halifax, Nova Scotia, people did not know how to react. As deadmau5 recalls, "I remember putting it on and looking out of the visor and seeing everyone in utter bewilderment. They were like, Who is this guy? Is he for real? But they warmed up to it real fast. When the lights came on in the helmet and . . . started blinking to the beat, the place went crazy."[67]

Today deadmau5 has six mau5heads, all of which he has designed. One of his favorites has a big LED screen wired to flash images in time with the music. The mouse heads are air conditioned and have screens inside that display software interfaces. And when it comes to his helmets, deadmau5 suffers for his art; his iconic mau5head with neon lights weighs more than 11 pounds (5 kg). But deadmau5 says it feels more like it weighs 100 pounds (45 kg) after jumping up and down during an hour-long set.

"Hydraulic and Monstrous"

By the time the album with the jokey title *Random Album Title* was released in late 2008, deadmau5's fame was rising rapidly. His collaboration with DJ Kaskade, "Move for Me," reached number one on the *Billboard* Dance/Mix Show Airplay chart, and his single "Ghosts 'n' Stuff" also hit number one on the dance charts. The video of "Ghosts 'n' Stuff," which shows deadmau5 dying and rising as a ghost, had attracted more than 37 million views on YouTube by 2015.

With his public profile growing rapidly, deadmau5 released a series of albums with humorous titles; *For Lack of a Better Name* (2009), *4X4=12* (2010), and *>album title goes here<* (2012). Music reviewer Louis Pattison describes the sounds on *>album title goes here<*: "From the snarky title to the oppressive robo-beat barrage that is his stock-in-trade, Zimmerman has the stance of

"Drugs Can Make It Much Worse"

Raves and EDM festivals have long been synonymous with drug use. Ravers often take psychoactive club drugs like LSD and MDMA, which is commonly referred to as Ecstasy (in pill form) or Molly (a powder). But deadmau5 might be one of the few sober people at his concerts, since drugs do not agree with him. He took LSD and Ecstasy a few times but had horrible, frightening experiences. Doctors diagnosed him with an unusual medical condition called neurocardiogenic syncope. This syndrome results in low blood pressure in the brain, which is worsened by club drugs. As deadmau5 explains: "My brain and my heart don't communicate the way they're supposed to. Drugs can make it much worse."

deadmau5 has other reasons to take an antidrug stance. He worries that outsiders might think his entire audience is composed of what he calls pill-popping kids. And he believes that the perceived link between EDM and drugs has had a negative effect on the music's popularity. The issue went public in 2012 after deadmau5 lambasted Madonna on Twitter for using drug lingo onstage at the Miami Ultra Music Festival. deadmau5's Twitter page blew up when people pointed out that many of his fans were on drugs. deadmau5 refused to change his attitude, saying it was insulting for others to associate harmful substances with the passion he puts into his music.

Quoted in Jonah Weiner, "From deadmau5 to Your House," *Rolling Stone*, February 17, 2011, p. 49.

a pugilist [boxer]. This in itself can be fairly impressive. 'Superliminal' and 'Channel 42' advance impassively, hydraulic and monstrous, crushing all in their path with insistent four-to-the-floor rhythm and heavy, saturated synth."[68]

Minimal Work, Maximum Profit

In 2013 deadmau5 earned around $21 million from album and merchandise sales and performance fees. That put him at number five on *Forbes* magazine's list of the world's highest-paid DJs. And this ranking was achieved while deadmau5 performed only 150 nights a year, about half as many shows as his peers Skrillex and Afrojack.

As one of the biggest names in EDM, deadmau5 has had his pick of collaborators, including the rock band Foo Fighters and the hip-hop group Cypress Hill. But as might be expected from someone who performs while wearing a mask, deadmau5 remains a loner. The doormat of his $1.5 million downtown Toronto penthouse reads: "YOU READ MY DOORMAT: THAT'S ENOUGH INTERACTION FOR ONE DAY."[69]

deadmau5 sees himself as an outsider in the rarified world of DJ superstars. In a 2014 interview with the *London Evening Standard*, he derided the label *EDM*, saying it stood for "Event-Driven Marketing" because of all the hype surrounding style. deadmau5 thinks many of his colleagues seem more inspired by money than music. EDM, he says, is "minimal work for maximum profit. . . . It's just really interesting to see that not too many people are forward-thinking about electronic music and they're just kinda like, 'Now, now, now, do it, do it, do it.'"[70] deadmau5 has even predicted that EDM will experience a massive collapse in popularity, something on the level of the crash of the disco fad in the late 1970s.

> "[EDM is] minimal work for maximum profit. . . . It's just really interesting to see that not too many people are forward-thinking about electronic music."[70]
>
> —deadmau5.

While dismissing the music that made him millions, deadmau5 also takes an antidrug stance in a scene where club drugs like MDMA (Ecstasy or Molly) are incredibly common. In 2012 he called pop superstar Madonna an idiot when she mentioned Molly from the stage while introducing Avicii at Miami's Ultra Music Festival. After the incident, deadmau5 wrote on his blog: "I'm not perfect but i do know that i am at the very least morally obligated not to blatantly inflict or advocate anything that's detrimental to society, others health, etc."[71]

For the Fans

Despite his prickly attitudes, deadmau5 continues to attract obsessive fans. They make mouse heads of their own and get tattoos of his company logo. deadmau5 stays in touch with his fans on social media: In 2015 he had 2.8 million followers on Twitter and 1 million on Instagram.

When deadmau5 released his seventh studio album, the double disc, twenty-five-track *while(1<2)*, he made it available for subscribers on his personal website. The album, which is close to two and a half hours long, features brooding piano pieces, gloomy electronica, and a Nine Inch Nails cover song. deadmau5 summed up his musical attitudes in a comment about the album: "It's not just about making a dance hit or the brand—I love engineering [all kinds of] music. . . . [On this album] I've done hip-hop tracks, glitch tracks, piano concertos, and dance hits. I think a large part of my fan base knows that, so this is for them."[72]

While deadmau5 reigns as an EDM icon, he remains a computer geek at heart. He likes to instant message with his mom, post clips of his rescue cat Professor Meowingtons on YouTube, and invent online games like *mau5ville*. And thanks to his mouse head masks, deadmau5 can walk down the street without anyone recognizing him. Whatever happens to the EDM scene in the future, odds are deadmau5 will be producing music long after the laser lights have faded from the stage.

CHAPTER 6

Calvin Harris

American pop music stars are some of the world's most celebrated performers. From Michael Jackson in the 1980s to Britney Spears in the 1990s and Beyoncé in the 2000s, pop singers have long dominated the lists of richest entertainers. But with the soaring popularity of DJs and EDM in the 2010s, that began to change. In 2015 one of the biggest moneymakers in the music world was Calvin Harris, a thirty-one-year-old DJ from Scotland.

According to *Forbes* magazine, Harris earned $66 million from live shows, merchandise and record sales, product endorsements, and outside business ventures. Harris's place on *Forbes*'s World's Highest-Paid Celebrities list shows that EDM has attained a striking new level of mainstream success. As the seventeenth-highest-paid celebrity in the world, Harris earned more money than pop singer Justin Timberlake ($63 million), rapper Jay Z ($56 million), and singer Beyoncé ($54.5 million). But unlike Timberlake and Beyoncé, who were huge stars when they were teenagers, Harris in his teen years was a loner who struggled in a series of low-wage jobs while dreaming of stardom.

"A Very Quiet Guy"

Calvin Harris was born Adam Richard Wiles on January 17, 1984, in the small town of Dumfries in southwestern Scotland. His father, David—a biochemist—and mother, Pamela—a homemaker—still live in the house where Adam grew up with his older sister, Sophie, and older brother, Edward.

Wiles's parents were born in Oxford, England, and Wiles picked up their English accent. As a youth, this made him a target for bullies who spoke with the more prevalent Scottish accent. To avoid his tormenters at Dumfries High School, Wiles spent his lunch periods in the music room. He learned music composition on a primitive Atari ST computer which ran *Notator*, an early music sequencing program.

At age fifteen, Wiles began to record original dance-pop compositions on a Commodore Amiga PC in his bedroom. After graduating high school, Wiles continued to write songs and record music but struggled to make a living. His first job was stocking shelves at a grocery store. He soon landed another job, gutting salmon at a fish-processing factory.

Wiles used most of his money to set up a home recording studio. For inspiration he purchased old vinyl records and used tape cassettes at a local music store. Owner Gordon Maxwell describes Wiles at the time: "He was always a very quiet guy, very reserved and very polite, and he was particularly interested in techno. He would come in with his DJ bag and fill it with 12-inch singles and head off again. He was a really nice guy and pretty chilled out, just very quiet really."[73]

> "[Calvin] was always a very quiet guy, very reserved and very polite, and he was particularly interested in techno. He would come in with his DJ bag and fill it with 12-inch singles and head off again."[73]
>
> —Gordon Maxwell, record store owner.

A "Racially Ambiguous" Name

In 2003, at age nineteen, Wiles moved to London to pursue his dream of becoming a singer, songwriter, and record producer. However, London has one of the most competitive music scenes in the world. Instead of making records, Wiles ended up working at another grocery store. Wiles, who is 6 feet 5 inches (196 cm) tall, later explained why he was good at his day job: "I'm really tall and could help old ladies reach their cans of beans."[74]

> "I thought Calvin Harris sounded a bit more racially ambiguous. I thought people might not know if I was black or not."[75]
>
> —Calvin Harris, DJ, songwriter, music producer.

Wiles wrote a number of songs while in London, but only one, "Let Me Know," found minor success; in 2004 the song appeared as a remix with vocalist Ayah on the Unabombers' live album *Electric Soul, Vol. 2*. Wiles decided a new name might help his career. What would help his career even more, he thought, was a name that caused listeners to think he was black. As Harris revealed in 2009: "My first single was more of a soul track, and I thought Calvin Harris sounded a bit more racially ambiguous. I thought people might not know if I was black or not. After that, I was stuck with it."[75]

Recording Hits at Home

The name change did little to improve his standing in the music world. Broke and dejected, Harris moved back to his parents' house in Dumfries in 2004. He took a job at the Marks & Spencer department and grocery store but continued to write and record music, posting numerous songs on the social network Myspace. In 2006 two of those songs, "Acceptable in the 80s" and "The Girls," attracted the attention of Mark Gillespie, a talent scout who had recently started a Myspace account. Harris's life changed overnight when Gillespie helped him land a contract with EMI, one of the largest record companies in the world. As Harris recalls: "I think within that month I signed a deal and I stacked my last chicken breast on the shelf of Marks & Spencer."[76]

"Acceptable in the 80s," which was a tribute to the electro, new wave, and synthpop music of the 1980s, helped forge Harris's trademark funky dance-pop sound. The song features irresistible hooks, fat staccato synths, crispy percussion, and a driving electro bass line. After its release in March 2007, "Acceptable in the

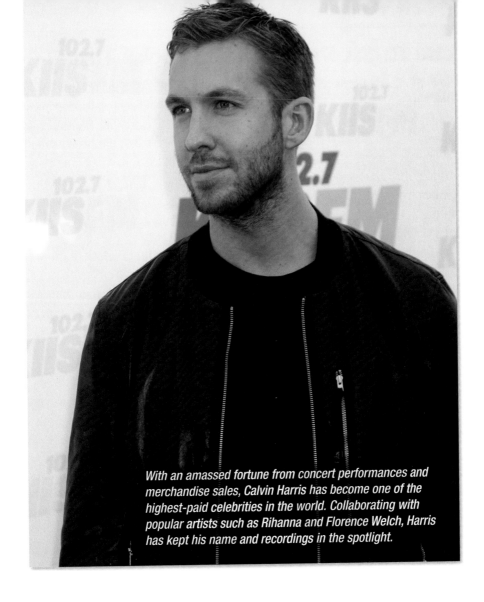

With an amassed fortune from concert performances and merchandise sales, Calvin Harris has become one of the highest-paid celebrities in the world. Collaborating with popular artists such as Rihanna and Florence Welch, Harris has kept his name and recordings in the spotlight.

80s" hit number ten on the UK Singles Chart and stayed there for nearly four months. "The Girls," which was released in June of the same year, was an even bigger hit, reaching number three.

Harris's hits were included on his 2007 debut album, *I Created Disco*, which featured a 1980s theme. The album was recorded entirely on Harris's ancient Amiga computer in his bedroom during the previous two years. Harris plays all the instruments and supplies the vocals for the album. *I Created Disco* debuted at number eight on the UK Albums Chart and eventually sold around 223,000 copies.

"The Right Place at the Right Time"

A line in the Calvin Harris hit song "We'll Be Coming Back" mentions riding a wave. Although the song is about a love affair, Harris rode a different kind of wave after the song was released; the explosive growth of EDM since 2012 coincided with Harris's cresting popularity. As Harris told *Forbes* in 2015: "The rise of dance music has been astronomical in the last three years. I happened to be in the right place at the right time."

Harris was referring to the swelling global value of EDM, which was around $6.9 billion in 2015. This was 50 percent more than in 2013. *Forbes*, which has been tracking DJ pay since 2012, says the total earnings of the top ten DJs grew from $125 million in 2012 to $274 million in 2014.

Harris has definitely been a beneficiary of this growth. He clocked more than 160 million streams on Spotify with his 2014 hit "Summer" and has achieved more than 1 billion song streams total. That kind of popularity has pushed Harris's DJ fees to more than $300,000 a night and made him one of the wealthiest entertainers on earth.

Quoted in Stephen Heyman, "An Unprecedented Success for Electronic Dance Music and Its D.J.s," *New York Times*, September 9, 2015. www.nytimes.com.

Dizzee Hits

Harris's connections at EMI helped him land a gig with Australian pop singer Kylie Minogue. In 2007 Harris cowrote and produced two songs for Minogue's tenth album, *X*. One of the songs, "In My Arms," also inspired by 1980s synthpop, received widespread critical acclaim and quickly rose to the top ten charts.

British rapper Dizzee Rascal loved "In My Arms" and came to Harris with an interesting proposition for a song called "Dance Wiv Me." Harris picks up the story: "Dizzee texted me saying he'd done this [vocal track] over someone else's music, but his verse was too good for their music, so could he do it with me instead? So I spent a long time on it, to make sure it lived up to his expectations. I sent him the track, and he called me at 2 in the morning to say it was amazing, so I knew it was good."[77]

Harris, who cowrote and sang on "Dance Wiv Me," was not alone in feeling good about it; the song topped the charts for a month and became Harris's first number one hit on the UK Singles Chart. With sales of more than six hundred thousand,

"Dance Wiv Me" went on to become the best-selling British single of 2008.

Pumping Disco and House Tracks

An EP version of "Dance Wiv Me" was included on Harris's next album, *Ready for the Weekend* (2009). With its driving beats, simple hooks, potent synth rushes, whooshes, and bleeps, *Ready for the Weekend* was an appropriately named party record. Reviewer Neil McCormick describes Harris's musical formula: "Songs start out simple and organic, introducing lyrical and melodic motifs that wouldn't sound out of place on a [rock] anthem, before opening up with some big synths into pumping disco and house tracks. . . . Harris handles vocal duties himself, stacking his smooth, plain voice with simple yet jazzy harmonies."[78]

By this time everything Harris touched turned to gold, and *Ready for the Weekend* was no exception. The album debuted at number one on both the UK Albums Chart and UK Dance Album Chart and spawned several hit singles.

Harris called *Ready for the Weekend* "stadium dance music,"[79] and he performed its songs at numerous stadiums during an extended 2010 tour of the United Kingdom, Ireland, the Netherlands, and the United States. However, after the whirlwind tour finished, Harris was tired of playing the role of a DJ who also sang lead vocals: "On one hand, I love to play football stadiums and see everyone with their hands in the air. On the other, I don't want to be a front man much longer. I'm not a natural singer, and I'd rather . . . use guest vocalists."[80]

> "Songs start out simple and organic, introducing lyrical and melodic motifs that wouldn't sound out of place on a [rock] anthem."[78]
>
> —Neil McCormick, music reviewer.

Collaborating with the Best

Harris did exactly that on his next album, *18 Months*, which debuted in 2012 and featured many top singers. Pop and R & B vocalist Rihanna sang on the Grammy-winning song "We Found

Love." The English indie pop artist Ellie Goulding added vocals to the top ten hit "I Need Your Love," and R & B artist Ne-Yo sang on the number one song "Let's Go." The breakout hit on *18 Months*, "Sweet Nothing," features the vocals of Florence Welch of the highly acclaimed English indie band Florence and the Machine.

18 Months produced eight top ten hits from a single album, a feat that placed Harris in the British record books. The previous record holder, pop superstar Michael Jackson, had seven top ten hits on two different albums: *Bad* (1987) and *Dangerous* (1991). *18 Months*, which sold more than 25 million singles in 2012, was also nominated for a Grammy for the Best Dance/Electronica Album, whereas Harris was nominated for Best British Male Solo Artist at the 2013 Brit Awards.

The international acclaim for *18 Months* helped make Harris the face of EDM. By 2013 he was performing more than 125 DJ gigs a year. Harris not only appeared at EDM-focused events like the Electric Daisy Carnival but at general music festivals such as the Coachella Valley Music and Arts Festival in California. Harris also earned more than $300,000 a night at Hakkasan, the biggest, most opulent EDM club in Las Vegas. Journalist Ryan Mac explains how Harris's dance-pop musical formula works well in a city more famous for gambling than dancing:

> Harris is able to command [$300,000 a night in Vegas] because of the crowd he attracts to clubs. With a DJ style that blends in stronger pop music elements than counterparts like deadmau5 . . . he's able to cater to both general admission crowd members and higher-spending bottle-service guests, who can spend tens of thousands of dollars for a table and a few bottles of champagne.[81]

Fireworks over the Ocean

The money kept pouring in after Harris released his fourth studio album *Motion* in October 2014. In many ways the album followed the pop formula Harris used on *18 Months*. Big-name collaborators included vocalists Goulding, Gwen Stefani, and Tinashe; rapper Big Sean; and the pop groups Haim, Hurts, and All About She. *Rolling Stone* placed *Motion* at number fifteen on its 20 Best

The meteoric rise of *18 Months* on the dance charts in 2012 brought Calvin Harris celebrity status and crossover appeal. Within a year, he was featured at the Electric Daisy Carnival (pictured) as well as more mainstream venues like the Coachella Valley Music and Arts Festival.

Pop Albums of 2014, writing: "Ellie Goulding's lovelorn warble prances forcefully down a string-draped runway on 'Outside,' Haim soars with 'Pray to God' . . . and Tinashe gives a welcome strut and slither to the bass-rattle of 'Dollar Signs.'"[82]

The biggest hit on *Motion* was the global smash "Summer," released as a single in April 2014. There was little surprise when the song, which debuted at number one in the United Kingdom, became the hit of the summer. The single sold more than 1 million copies in the United States alone by July. Sailing along at 128 bpm, "Summer" features Harris on vocals, backed by his distinctive massive synth hooks. As *Rolling Stone* wrote, the song "unfolds like a fireworks display over the ocean."[83]

Pop Music and a Good Haircut

Motion shared the 20 Best Pop Albums list with Taylor Swift's *1989*. And the two music industry giants were found together beyond the pages of *Rolling Stone*. Harris and Swift began dating in early 2015, and the couple quickly became a constant presence in the tabloid press. By the end of the year, the two were denying marriage rumors.

Calvin Harris and Taylor Swift

Calvin Harris and pop superstar Taylor Swift started dating in March 2015. Fans of both stars were thrilled when Harris posted pictures of Swift's cats on Instagram along with her cooking vegan barbeque at home. Swift has had numerous failed relationships with celebrities, including Harry Styles, Zac Efron, and Jake Gyllenhaal. However, author Douglas Wight believes Swift's relationship with Harris may be more lasting:

> Harris is older and wiser and he's not seduced by celebrity. . . . In the past Taylor has gone out with young stars like Joe Jonas and Harry Styles, who get their heads turned by having a famous girlfriend. Harris is not like that, he's down to earth, his head is screwed on. Hopefully Taylor won't be writing any new songs about heartbreak. In Harris, [I] think she has found the perfect boyfriend. He gave up alcohol in 2008, he doesn't do drugs, he works hard and is totally down to earth.

Quoted in Alexander Lerche and Annette Witheridge, "How Taylor Swift's DJ Main Squeeze Calvin Harris Gutted Scottish Salmon for the Queen, Stacked Supermarket Shelves and Got a Makeover to Launch His $100 Million Career," *Daily Mail* (London), May 11, 2015. www.dailymail.co.uk.

In June *Forbes* took notice of the relationship between Harris and Swift; the financial magazine ranked the duo as the highest-paid celebrity couple in the world, with combined earnings of more than $146 million. With this designation, the thirty-one-year-old Harris and twenty-five-year-old Swift knocked Jay Z and Beyoncé from the number one spot they had occupied for years.

Despite this lofty position in the public eye, by all accounts Harris is a down-to-earth artist who places a greater value on his music than on wealth and fame. Harris started out gutting fish by day and recording songs by night. He honestly assessed his own talents and was unafraid to collaborate with singers who added excellence to his songs. As a reward, Harris's songs have earned more than 1 billion plays on Spotify. As to the secret of his success, Harris reveals: "Pop music comes naturally to me—it's what I do every day. . . . Oh, and I also got a good haircut. I used to have a terrible haircut."[84]

SOURCE NOTES

Introduction: Beats and Heartbeats

1. Quoted in Songfacts, "Where It's At by Beck," 2015. www.song facts.com.
2. Bernardo Alexander Attias, Anna Gavanas, and Hillegonda C. Rietveld, eds., *DJ Culture in the Mix*. New York: Bloomsbury, 2013, pp. 23–24.
3. Quoted in Attias et al., *DJ Culture in the Mix*, p. 21.
4. Quoted in Erick, "Moby Breaks Down Some of the Terminology of Electronic Dance Music," Electrowow, December 15, 2011. www.electrowow.net.
5. Quoted in Erick, "Moby Breaks Down Some of the Terminology of Electronic Dance Music."
6. Attias et al., *DJ Culture in the Mix*, p. 1.

Chapter 1: Avicii

7. Quoted in Patrick Doyle, "Avicii's Rave New World," *Rolling Stone*, August 16, 2013. www.rollingstone.com.
8. Quoted in Alejandra Loera, "Avicii: In Buddhism It Means the Lowest Level of Hell," *OC Weekly* (blog), April 19, 2012. http://blogs.ocweekly.com.
9. Quoted in Spin Artist Agency, "Avicii," 2015. www.spinartistagency.com.
10. Quoted in Jessica Pressler, "The King of Oontz Oontz Oontz," *GQ*, March 29, 2013. www.gq.com.

11. Payal Patel, "Swedish DJ Avicii Takes the World by Storm," AXS, August 16, 2014. www.axs.com.

12. Quoted in Pressler, "The King of Oontz Oontz Oontz."

13. Quoted in Pressler, "The King of Oontz Oontz Oontz."

14. Quoted in Pressler, "The King of Oontz Oontz Oontz."

15. Quoted in Pressler, "The King of Oontz Oontz Oontz."

16. Quoted in Dan Hyman, "Flo Rida and Avicii Remember Etta James," *Rolling Stone*, January 24, 2012. www.rollingstone.com.

17. Elliot Alpern, "Avicii Rocks Crowded Dance Floor at Consol Energy Center," *Pittsburgh Post-Gazette*, June 15, 2012. www.post-gazette .com.

18. Quoted in Doyle, "Avicii's Rave New World."

19. Philip Sherburne, "EDM Superstar Avicii Made a Kazoo-Heavy Kinda-Country Record with 'True,' It's Awesome," *Spin*, September 12, 2013. www.spin.com.

20. Sherburne, "EDM Superstar Avicii Made a Kazoo-Heavy Kinda-Country Record with 'True,' It's Awesome."

21. Quoted in Pressler, "The King of Oontz Oontz Oontz."

22. Quoted in Doyle, "Avicii's Rave New World."

Chapter 2: Annie Mac

23. Annie Mac, "Annie Mac: Stop Asking Me Questions About Being a Woman," Thump, November 13, 2014. https://thump.vice.com.

24. Quoted in Hardfest, "Annie Mac," 2011. http://artists.hardfest.com.

25. Quoted in Queen's University Belfast, "Annie Mac: My Time at Queen's," 2015. www.qub.ac.uk.

26. Quoted in Queen's University Belfast, "Annie Mac."

27. Quoted in *Resident Advisor*, "Annie Mac," 2015. www.resident advisor.net.

28. Quoted in Queen's University Belfast, "Annie Mac."

29. Quoted in *Resident Advisor*, "Annie Mac."

30. Quoted in Michelle Kambasha, "Everybody Wants to Be a DJ: Annie Mac," Clash, December 12, 2012. www.clashmusic.com.

31. Annie Mac, "Life on the Touring Frontline," Thump, December 3, 2013. https://thump.vice.com.

32. Mac, "Annie Mac."

33. Quoted in BBC, "Annie Mac Confirmed as New Presenter of Radio 1's Weekday Evening Show," February 15, 2015. www.bbc.co.uk.

34. Quoted in Kambasha, "Everybody Wants to Be a DJ."

Chapter 3: Afrojack

35. Quoted in Dan Hyman, "Afrojack on His Debut Album, His Hair and Working with Friends," *Rolling Stone*, March 3, 2012. www.rolling stone.com.
36. Quoted in David Marchese, "Exclusive: Afrojack Announces Debut Album 'Forget the World,'" *Rolling Stone*, March 13, 2014. www .rollingstone.com.
37. Quoted in Maarten van Rossem, "Afrojack, Businessman Between Underground and Mainstream," *Maarten!*, February 19, 2013. www.maartenonline.nl.
38. Quoted in Akshay Bhansali, "Afrojack Says Eva Simons Shines in 'Take Over Control' Video," MTV News, November 9, 2010. www .mtv.com.
39. Shahryar Rizvi, "The Problem with . . . Pitbull's 'Give Me Everything' (Feat. Ne-Yo, Afrojack, Nayer)," *Dallas Observer*, July 28, 2011. www.dallasobserver.com.
40. Quoted in Ryan Mac, "DJ Wars: Inside the Las Vegas Battles for the World's Top Electronic Music Talent," *Forbes*, August 14, 2013. www.forbes.com.
41. Quoted in Marchese, "Exclusive.'"
42. Quoted in Molly Hankins, "Afrojack Introduces His Daughter to the World," BPM, October 10, 2013. www.thebpm.net.
43. Quoted in Van Rossem, "Afrojack, Businessman Between Underground and Mainstream."
44. Quoted in Dan Hyman, "Afrojack: 'I Want My Grandma to Understand' My Music," *Rolling Stone*, April 14, 2012. www.rollingstone .com.

Chapter 4: Skrillex

45. Robert Ker, "Concert Review: With Bass 'Drops' and Showmanship, Skrillex Entertains," *Portland* (Maine) *Press Herald*, August 19, 2014. www.pressherald.com.
46. Jonah Weiner, "The Boy Inside the Beat," *Rolling Stone*, March 27, 2014, p. 36.
47. Quoted in Weiner, "The Boy Inside the Beat," p. 38.
48. Quoted in Weiner, "The Boy Inside the Beat," p. 38.
49. Quoted in James C. McKinley Jr., "Manic Peter Pan Rules Dance Clubs," *New York Times*, January 26, 2012. www.nytimes.com.
50. Weiner, "The Boy Inside the Beat," pp. 38–39.

51. Quoted in McKinley, "Manic Peter Pan Rules Dance Clubs."

52. Joe DeAndrea, "Sonny Moore-Gypsyhook EP," AbsolutePunk.net, April 7, 2009. http://absolutepunk.net.

53. Quoted in Priya Elan, "30 Things You Should Know About Skrillex," NME, February 20, 2012. www.nme.com.

54. Quoted in Neil Strauss, "Skrillex: Eight Wild Nights and Busy Days with the Superstar," *Rolling Stone*, March 1, 2012. www.rolling stone.com.

55. Max Paradise, "Skrillex: Scary Monsters and Nice Sprites," Sputnik Music, December 8, 2010. www.sputnikmusic.com.

56. Quoted in McKinley, "Manic Peter Pan Rules Dance Clubs."

57. Quoted in Joe Muggs, "Is Skrillex the Most Hated Man in Dubstep?," *Guardian* (Manchester), September 29, 2011. www.the guardian.com.

58. Quoted in Muggs, "Is Skrillex the Most Hated Man in Dubstep?"

59. Quoted in Muggs, "Is Skrillex the Most Hated Man in Dubstep?"

Chapter 5: deadmau5

60. Joel Zimmerman, "deadmau5," deadmau5, 2015. www.dead mau5.com.

61. Quoted in Jonah Weiner, "From deadmau5 to Your House," *Rolling Stone*, February 17, 2011, p. 49.

62. Quoted in Weiner, "From deadmau5 to Your House," p. 49.

63. Quoted in DJ List, "deadmau5," 2015. http://thedjlist.com.

64. Quoted in Weiner, "From deadmau5 to Your House," p. 49.

65. Zimmerman, "deadmau5."

66. Zimmerman, "deadmau5."

67. Zimmerman, "deadmau5."

68. Louis Pattison, ">*album title goes here*<," BBC Music, September 24, 2012. www.bbc.co.uk.

69. Quoted in Weiner, "From deadmau5 to Your House," p. 48.

70. Quoted in Kat Bein, "deadmau5: EDM Is Commercial Crap, Just an Acronym for 'Event-Driven Marketing,'" *Miami New Times*, November 28, 2012. www.miaminewtimes.com.

71. Quoted in Sean Michaels, "deadmau5 Accuses Madonna of Ecstasy Reference at Ultra Music Festival," *Guardian* (Manchester), March 27, 2012. www.theguardian.com.

72. Joel Zimmerman, "While(1<2)," deadmau5, 2015. www.deadmau5 .com.

Chapter 6: Calvin Harris

73. Quoted in Alexander Lerche and Annette Witheridge, "How Taylor Swift's DJ Main Squeeze Calvin Harris Gutted Scottish Salmon for the Queen, Stacked Supermarket Shelves and Got a Makeover to Launch His $100 Million Career," *Daily Mail* (London), May 11, 2015. www.dailymail.co.uk.
74. Quoted in *Belfast Telegraph*, "Calvin Harris: I Worked in a Fish Factory," October 29, 2012. www.belfasttelegraph.co.uk.
75. Quoted in Mayer Nissim, "Harris 'Wanted Racially Ambiguous Name,'" Digital Spy, August 13, 2009. www.digitalspy.com.
76. Quoted in Ryan Mac, "EDM's $46 Million Man: How Calvin Harris Became the World's Highest-Paid DJ," *Forbes*, August 13, 2013. www.forbes.com.
77. Quoted in DJ List, "Calvin Harris," 2015. http://thedjlist.com.
78. Neil McCormick, "Calvin Harris: Ready for the Weekend, Pop CD of the Week," *Telegraph* (London), August 6, 2009. www.telegraph.co.uk.
79. Quoted in McCormick, "Calvin Harris."
80. Quoted in Adrian Thrills, "I Had to Get Drunk with Kylie: Dance DJ Calvin Harris on Meeting His Idols … and Stacking Shelves at Safeway," *Daily Mail* (London), August 9, 2009. www.dailymail.co.uk.
81. Mac, "EDM's $46 Million Man."
82. *Rolling Stone*, "20 Best Pop Albums of 2014," December 19, 2014. www.rollingstone.com.
83. *Rolling Stone*, "20 Best Pop Albums of 2014."
84. Quoted in Tim Jonze, "Calvin Harris: The Secrets of My Success," *Guardian* (Manchester), December 21, 2012. www.theguardian.com.

FOR FURTHER RESEARCH

Books

Joseph Beasley, *Few Other Afrojack Titles Offer So Much—186 Facts*. Brisbane, Australia: Emereo, 2015.

Alison Eldridge and Stephen Eldridge, *Investigate Club Drugs*. New York: Enslow, 2014.

Rebekah Farrugia, ed., *Beyond the Dance Floor: Female DJs, Technology, and Electronic Dance Music Culture*. Chicago: Intellect, 2012.

Adam Salas, *Calvin Harris: 270 Success Facts*. Brisbane, Australia: Emereo, 2014.

Douglas Wight, *Calvin Harris*. Edinburgh: Black and White, 2015.

Internet Sources and Websites

Annie Mac Presents (http://anniemacpresents.com). This site is hosted by the influential BBC DJ Annie Mac and features the hottest new DJs emerging from the EDM scene. The site includes excerpts from Mac's BBC Radio 1 show, podcasts, videos, and blogs.

Beatport (www.beatport.com). Beatport is considered the iTunes of the EDM scene, and this site contains thousands of songs and popular videos by DJs from all over the world. Links include upcoming EDM shows with a focus on local gigs.

deadmau5 (www.deadmau5.com). This website shows deadmau5 working in the studio, features official videos, and lets users participate in the DJ's private social network, Twitch, where they can chat while checking out his latest broadcast. There is also a link to the deadmau5 Coffee Runs website, where the DJ drives around with other DJs and visits coffee shops.

DJ List (http://thedjlist.com). The DJ List is the leading resource for global DJ information online. As the world's largest DJ directory, the list has been providing DJ and EDM information since 1997. Information includes biographies of DJs, record labels, clubs, agents, and DJ List RADIO, which allows users to listen to electronic dance music sorted by genre, trending, local DJs, and favorites.

Calvin Harris (www.calvinharris.co.uk/gb/home). Harris's visually stunning website reflects his impact as the world's highest-paid DJ. Videos, tweets, Instagram uploads, concert dates, and the latest music are all part of the website's flash.

March of the Afrojack (www.youtube.com). This YouTube video produced by Afrojack is a documentary about the superstar DJ's life, featuring his childhood roots, his rise to fame, backstage footage, and the artist talking about his daughter, Vegas.

Resident Advisor (www.residentadvisor.net). *Resident Advisor* was established in 2001 as an online music magazine and community platform dedicated to showcasing electronic music, artists, and events around the globe. The site features news, reviews, event listings, clubs, photos, artists, charts, and podcasts geared toward music fans, club goers, DJs, producers, venue owners, promoters, and record labels.

Skrillex (www.skrillex.com). The official website of "SONNY—BOOM BOOM BAT," better known as Skrillex, provides everything users need to know about the dubstep king. Links take fans to the DJ's Soundcloud postings, videos, and photos, as well as his Instagram, Facebook, and Twitter uploads.

Thump (www.thump.vice.com). This website, hosted by the HBO TV series *Vice*, chronicles global dance music culture, focusing on the music, artists, and fans. The site contains original videos from dance events around the globe, breaking news, and exclusive mixes from renowned DJs.

Your EDM (www.youredm.com). With more than 4 million monthly visitors, YourEDM.com delivers free downloads, music, videos, and up-to-date news related to the EDM scene. Music is divided into genres and subgenres, including house, future house, new disco, bass, dubstep, trance, and trouse.

INDEX

PICTURE CREDITS